Cosmic Breath:
Poetry of the Universe

KAREN NEVERLAND

ISBN-13: 978-0615880624 (Neverland Publications)
ISBN-10: 0615880622

AUTHOR'S NOTE

In 2012 and 2013, I erased most of my poetry as an exercise in impermanence. This is what remains.

Thank you to the Greenhouse Effect Café community. When Sean Armstrong died in 2009, I took over hosting the Greenhouse Effect Open, a community based open microphone. The family and friends I found there shaped me and my poetry in ways I may never understand.

Thank you to family—chosen and given—for your support and companionship on this epic journey.

Thank you most of all to the Great Cosmic Breath.

CONTENTS

1. Cosmic Breath

On the inhale, God created Themselves.
On the exhale, all of creation.

We are Cosmic Breath manifest.
We are whispers of the Divine into universal eardrums.
We are the microcosmic cycle of life and death assembled into
   breath.

When we forget to breathe, we forget our souls.
Our lungs are throbbing in withdrawal, swallowing our hearts in
   swollen separation from airstreams.
There is a shallow-breath epidemic arresting and suffocating us.
Empty lungs are choking on themselves.
We are drowning while only ankle deep in the Life Pool's current.

Stop everything until you remember how to breathe.
Meditation is the remembrance of Breath.
Breath is the remembrance of Life.
Life is the remembrance of Infinity.
We are no more or less than the air that moves through us.
When we all breathe in unison, the world knows peace.

Remember the inhale:
Capture the Earth's whirlwinds and bring them into vast jungle lungs.
Experience flower-petal rungs bursting into bloom as the rainforest
   flourishes.
Crystallize tropical waves into gemstones.
Taste the unique flavor of each cotton-candy, oxygen cloud in
   ecstasy.
Line the ribs with unsaid words of magic-spell scrolls, rolled on
   marshmallow paper.
Feel the expansion of chest.
The expansion of breath.
The expansion of mind to find the secret to rooted reality and being.
Stretch out… Spread out… Reach out—

like a candle, release this sublime glory.

Remember the exhale:
Liberate lungs of extracted plant placenta.
Neutralize the poison trapped within.
Free the spirit from the unified inside of the body.
Shatter glittering gemstones that gilded sides.
Deliver the last bit of breath to the cosmos.
Surrender to the truth of eternal sleep again and again and again—
And again.

Each exhale is a step away from death; do not fear it.
We are the karmic cycle of re-breath.
Respiration is the Great Figure Eight we never escape from.
Breathing is the most pure form of Creation and Destruction.
Exhalations form words into mini *dues ex machinas*—slaves that toil in
    mines(minds) long after we have gone.
But to create whispers into language, we must self-destruct the
    dynamite of our life-force into them.

True Breathing transcends speaking:
There are no words for the immortal nature of Bliss.
It is impossible to breathe and speak at the same time.
Why are so many crafting tongues into shrieking falcons?
Silence is humanity's long lost ex-lover.

At any moment we will exhale from here and inhale somewhere else.
Dreams are the practice of this, the practice of death.
In our Last Inhalation, may we all experience the luxury of dying in
    Silence.
Holding on to that final cycle in consciousness until we merge back
    into the Eternal Cosmic Breath.   *—Spring 2010*

2. SHHH...

Sometimes... most times... and all times...
I am lost in my mind's monotonous monologue of thought and I
    find that the truth of Experience is often forgotten.
There's Experience, Existence, Consciousness, and Now and they are
    all tied together somehow.
More than my mind will ever allow.
I've thrown away Time and held onto things because objects bring
    tangibility to my hands and eyes.
I've latched onto lies that scream fallacy because they seem to be
    easy.

This world keeps changing, exchanging itself for the visions in our
    heads, but instead of viewing Heaven, we fear a future hell.
And our dwelling is compelling the world to transform into an
    unlivable realm, unreal—void of the emotions we long to feel.
But what if this is Heaven, and when you die you're done?
Actuality is more overwhelming than any religious or political
    conspiracy can ever be.
The nonsensical dominates all I see: It seems Dr. Seuss stories are
    closer to Reality.
Oh! I wish there was a Lorax speaking for the trees, because each
    Earth piece chopped down drifts around in my bloodstream and
    dams up in my heart.
Damn my heart!
This world is falling apart faster than I want to fix it.
Our hate seems legitimate since we're all just victims of other victims
    anyway.
The world brims with our dimming flames within and perpetuates
    more hate with all the fillers we pile in.
Yet, at least dormant Love explodes every so often and prevents us
    from flat-lining.

I suspect the truths about Love are catching, but many still look for
    Joy in escapism.
We leave the gift-wrap on the Present and then abandon it under a
    wilting heart tree to wait... Wait... Wait...
Our hearts are growing heavy with wait(weight)!

We save time with modern day devices, then happily pay the prices of
electronic media liars, literally spending our lives to watch
television, where *our* desires are enjoyed by others.
When will we realize that the world is in our eyes?
Instead we look outside in things and hang our own noose swings
with all we buy.
Life passes us by, and still we buy, buy, buy, continually tied in more
lies, distracting us from what we really want.
The more we think, the less we Be.
And really, I just want to learn to love freely and experience this
world completely.

And sometimes… most times… and all times…
I am struggling to un-bury the Me inside and listen to Her.
Listen *for* Her.
Hear my Inner Sage as I peer at the Universe in a grain of sand and
finally understand it.
I guess we're on the right path because it means we've never been
here before.
Therefore we're traveling in a new direction, traveling in the Now
direction.
To my recollection that's all there is.
Maybe God stopped talking because we stopped listening.
Listen:

When was the last time you remember listening?

I guess the only answers I have are:
Go breathe in that air, because it's getting less and less likely that it
will be there tomorrow, because there is no Lorax speaking for
the trees and the longer you wait to Be, the less likely it is to be
free.
Oh, and don't forget to listen for the Music.
God speaks in Music.
Your heart is a drum, your breath is the wind section, and with blood
veins as strings and a soul that screams, you have everything you
need to sing dreams.
You have everything you need to change things.
But you have to Listen first.   —*Fall 2009*

3. Dissonance

I love the person hidden in your chest cavity:
The small, soft, secretive figure tucked away in the ribcage cave of
    your torso.
A velveteen covered character that steadily spins spinning wheel
    circles from your heart and sometimes pricks the finger of
    enchanted sleeping beauties.
The tiny figure that itches to escape, but only sometimes presents
    himself when good soul-scratchers are near.

I love the pulsing pigments of your precious inner paintbrush:
The true artisan of life that owns secrets on cascading canvases that
    are covered with the colors of the World Soul.
I hear the forgotten libraries of stashed-away sonnets and mystic
    tomes in the tones of ancient serenades that are available in your
    eyes, for those with open ears.

There's a creature flowing through your veins:
A celestial serpent that slithers to the beat of your seductive smile.
A creature like a moth that draws the flame to itself rather than flying
    into the illumination and flirts with danger through breaths that
    whisper like wings on the wind.

There's a dancer drifting in your mind:
The exotic display of wit of one unafraid of being locked in by
    circumstance.
The enticing taste of your witty silver-tongue is my favorite flavor.

I love the feeling of your soul as it sifts through the sieve of my outer
    shell and into the depths of my inner elixir, changing the potion
    with only a sliver of your alchemy-composed kisses.
You're like a shadow that stalks my every step even when the Sun has
    sunken from the sky, by leaving wet sidewalk footprints on my
    every thought.
You know, I could find rhymes for everything I love about you.
I could... but the truth is:
They are all just miniscule manifestations of the song singing in your
    center.

And no matter what the outer presentation of that person is or does,
   and no matter how much it hurts sometimes:
I am in love with the silken-string chords as well as the dissonance
   that resonates in your heart.   —*Spring 2009*

4. I Choose Music

I fell in love while lost halfway between the two-day-old makeup and
  a couple days' starvation.
Nothing happened, yet our lives were being systematically broken
  down and destroyed.
We were realizing the truths of sex, drugs, and rock 'n' roll.
We were living lives too full of reverberating madness.
We were dying deaths too full of Love.
Our hearts were pulsing so hard that sapphires bled from our pores.
We cried as the flesh was ripped open and gems were delivered.
It took extreme agony to claw the sparkling ideas from our bodies,
  but the result was a seductive melody from a siren's golden harp
  strings.
We traveled toward the maddening disaster of ourselves, but the
  iridescent crystals were worth every little misfortune.
So we made our way forward and never looked back.

The world was changing and we were just trying to find an edge
  worth balancing on.
Fighting in the old system for a new system.
Living in the new system while our old-system ways were dying
  within us.
Meanwhile, the world was changing.

We kept on singing because we wanted to forget our repressed
  silence and force the whole restricted world to forget theirs.
We kept on playing because we couldn't stop the perpetuating,
  perplexing hope that beat through every moment we had.
The passion rode us long and hard and we never regretted a second.
The world was changing.

There were romances in the sky and blues in our hearts.
There were happy endings and fresh new starts.
The planet was merging and we were challenged to rise above a
  somnambulist, sequestered existence.
To reinvent, rediscover, and renovate ourselves.
Challenged to experience everything we can envision, but are afraid
  to show to the other surrendered souls.

We suffered with sick, sore, and melted hearts.
Fighting our way through the questions, while dreading the answers,
and drying up inside.
But somehow, the inkwells overflowed and we expressed everything
in the end.

Somewhere between the all-nighters and the sleepless indecision.
Somewhere in the drunken exploration of our darkest sides.
Somewhere in the rotten discovery of evident ideas and confusing
realities.
Between the things we hated in ourselves and despised about the
world.
Somewhere in there, I fell out of love with myself.
And fell in love with the overwhelming and unexplained music of
Life.   —*Winter 2008-09*

5. Personal Body Bag

Alcohol is an unseen scorpion waiting at the foot of the bed.
It will crawl up your spine-train and sting you in the brain when you
    go to sleep.
It's a truth serum that turns even the most cautious from Dr. Jekyll to
    Hyde.
To hide you from anything you're afraid of with the sweet release of
    forgetful bliss.
But returned sobriety highlights the truth with a bright yellow marker
    and plasters it on the billboard mind-ads as soon as the inner eyes
    are functioning again.

Alcohol is a detailed escape plan for those who want to run away
    from themselves:
An unbreakable chrysalis.
A knife at your throat.
A bear trap at the foot of a blind man.
She's a bitchy but beautiful temptress you want to fuck over and
    over:
Flipping through your inner thoughts until she finds exactly what she
    needs to manipulate you.
Offering just enough escape to make the jailbreak worthwhile.
Offering a boat with a hole just small enough to stay afloat, but a
    boat that will never go anywhere or accomplish anything.

She douses your inner flame with buckets of fermented pleasure,
    until there's only the spark of a person left.
Leaving the glimmer of a soul, but distorting the rest with unburnable
    liquid retardant that flows quickly through the bloodstream.
Replacing the natural molecular structure with chemicals because the
    blacked-out beast is "more likable" than the sober one.
But the drunk person you call free is actually weighed down with
    your own body bag.
Being dragged by your own drugged-up abuses and fears toward the
    East River.
Shot after alcoholic shot of cement shoe-casings strapped to your
    ankles as you throw yourself into an ocean of bottled escape.

But the levels have risen above your head and there's more there than
you could ever hope to drink.
There are more lies than you could ever run out of.
There are more excuses than you'll ever need to convince anyone but
yourself.
It's easy to be happy when you don't take anyone into consideration,
except for your next drink.
It's easy to keep yourself confused when there are no free moments
to realize how fragile your constructed character is.

How do I show you that all you have to do is un-strap the cement
shoes, shred your excuse-marked plan, cut the caterpillar casing,
and fly above the knife that holds you ransom?
How do I show the misguided, damaged person you've so quickly
discarded where the trail is, when you refuse to understand that
you are even lost, let alone ask for directions?
How do I trade in the false delusion-drinker for the real dream-seeker
that burns inside?
And not with the burn of alcohol—the burn of a Life Flame so hot it
ignites magma fireballs in every passing person.

Listen: I'm not saying drinking is wrong.
Or that you should stop altogether.
Only that it's an easy costume to put on when you're afraid of what's
under the mask.
The more you practice being the character of that deception, the
harder it is to reveal the beautiful naked skin beneath.
It's impossible to dream when your mind has to relearn how to walk.
It's impossible to feel alive when your body has to filter out poisons
and remember how to breathe.
It's impossible to love others when you're hiding from yourself.

My friends, there's a line between when a substance enhances life and
when it becomes life.
You can cross it if you need to.
I've been there; I understand that need.
I'll be waiting for you when you decide to come back.
With a gasoline tank of fuel and as many matches as we need to
relight your soul.   *—Spring 2009*

6. Twelve-Step Program

There are many people looking toward the end of the human race in
an almost excited anticipation.
They watch our negative qualities, counting them up one by one, and
declare our impending destruction.
I don't understand this.
I've tried to see the world the way the news explains, but there must
be something wrong with me, because I just don't get their
description.
I've never seen one human kill another and it seems unreal to me.
I'm not saying that terrible things don't exist: It's just that I can't
believe the dramatized television projection either.
I can't understand war and poverty by watching them on a screen; in
fact, I feel more apathetic when I try to.
I'd rather base life off of what I have seen, than on a false image
funded by money.
You see, to me, the world is different—full of magic.
I wish I could share it with you, but there are no words to explain
being alive.
I suppose I can only describe a few concepts and hope something
clicks.
So here are my *Twelve Steps to Awareness*:

1. I live in a world of doorways. With every step, I exit one place and
   enter somewhere new. I don't dwell on which way I walked, or
   how I went about turning the doorknob. I just enjoy the new
   place I've now entered into.

2. I eat a lot of carrots, because I like the way they hide under the
   ground; it's like a secret. And yet, when you uproot them, they
   look like exactly what they are—a root. And that irony of honesty
   and secrecy, tickles me, and I can't help but laughing when I eat
   them.

3. I love clichés, because the best things in life are overdone, and
   that's because they are the best things in life! We all eventually
   stumble upon the same amazing things and that doesn't make you
   any less unique. In fact, it makes you more so, because you found

the same thing in an entirely different way, on an entirely different path. Besides, crying has been done the same way for ages and that is the very definition of cliché, but it never gets less powerful when done wholeheartedly.

4. Sex is just a rhythm. There's no sin in movement. I love the way the pulse of in and out pushes my body up and down. It's one of the few times when heart, body, and mind are united in a steady pulse. And since everything in existence is moving in a constant flow, sex is just us joining into that movement of the Universe.

5. I come alive in embarrassing situations because I can hear my ego dying in my head as it struggles against the fabric it's woven itself out of. Ego death allows room for my true voice to come through, so I embrace anything that makes "me" feel smaller, because in reality: It's making Me bigger.

6. I memorize people's eyes and keep track of how the weather affects their color.

7. My closest friends talk to the Moon because they are not afraid to speak to inanimate objects openly, even if that means that they're crazy. Besides, the Moon is hardly inanimate: She moves greater distances in a day than we will know in a lifetime.

8. Trees grow through sidewalks, power lines, and metal foundations. They keep growing when we chop off their arms and they keep living even when totally confined—think of a Bonsai tree. This is how we were meant to live. And only we are stopping ourselves.

9. I act childish in adult situations, I make things up regularly, and I specialize in immaturity. When did we all become so *grown up* anyway? For all I know, the Bible had it right and we become adults at 500-years-old. The world looks pretty impressive when you realize it's run by children.

10. I spend most of my time sober. Coffee, alcohol, and drugs are fun, but nothing makes me feel alive like conscious breathing does. Don't get me wrong, there's a place for *everything* in

moderation. But no amount of fun feels as surreal as knowing that I'm alive—Right Now. Life is a string of "Right Nows" and I don't want to break the chain because I'm not paying attention. If you wonder why life is passing you by, you might want to try being an active participant in it.

11. I spend time figuring out how negative qualities are actually positives. Like how obesity rates make America most likely to survive the next ice age apocalypse... Or how suffering is the sole cause of growth and dying allows room for new life. This is worthy use of my time. I wouldn't take back a moment, not for an entire lifetime of new ones.

12. I often see myself in other people. Even more incredible: I often see others inside of myself. I first understood Infinity when I could look at every person I met and know that my heart already contained a place for them. It brings new meaning to the phrase: "I am Everything."

This is my twelve-step program, the only way I can explain it.
I know there is hardship in the world, and I feel for it, but I think more than our sympathy, the world just needs a new vision.
I guess I'm a romantic, but happiness is a perspective you choose.
It doesn't "happen" to you.
If we can all realign our eyes to the surreal world that surrounds us, perhaps we'll have a chance to see a little more for a little longer.
Nothing lasts forever, but it'd be a shame to see such grace disintegrate away, though it very well may.
So, if you get tired of the pessimistic perspective, feel free to focus on Beauty with me.
Remember, you're already in my heart, and there's always room for you to start believing in what you're seeing.
My final advice:
Focus on the dream, and you'll realize you're sleeping.
Until then, I'll keep looking for you in your eyes, each time the weather changes.
And I'll keep leaving these steps along the way, as I simply *follow* the steps that came before me.   —*Winter 2010-11*

7. Through the Rabbit Hole

Childhood was composed of mud pies, Cheez Whiz, and backyard
    adventures:
Mountainside extravaganzas stole whole days away, replacing them
    with earthy fabricated memories worming through my brain.
Each day was a swing set creaking from endless play:
Forward and back, up and down, non-stop overexertion expecting
    every second to be my last on this planet.
Because my child-mind knew that at any moment—
These spaceships are due back on the Moon and I didn't want to
    leave before I'd explored this world fully.

I spent childhood running away from reality.
The fantasy of flying forced me on the ground more often than not,
    but I always made it back up before my mind had time to
    convince me I'd failed.
My visions were created from the concrete and scraped knees, and
    they were more powerful than anything the adults could tell me.
I hid away in the imaginary:
Cement tunnels were an entrance to the Land of Oz, Wonderland,
    and mystical Narnia.
Places where Time did not exist and I was a fairy princess who kissed
    frogs and found her prince on any given day.
They call this "child's play," but those cloud-vapor dragons are more
    real to me than the world the adults are peddling.

In their world, "poli-ticks" have infested the heads of the people.
There's a Wicked Witch in the West killing Munchkins for a pair of
    ruby slippers.
In their story, the land is held in the clutches of the Queen of Hearts:
"Off with your heads! You don't need them to paint the roses red."
Just spend your day as a slave to the leaders' game of croquet.
Their wild hedges have been trimmed into neat little cubical cages.
There is no way to climb back through the rabbit hole.
They call this reality?
This world is more imagined than a story.
Can you blame me for not believing in it?
My ideas are more concrete than all of their endless sidewalks.

The tendency to fall into dreams may be escapism, but it is less of a
  prison than the bars the world places on expression.
I remember finding lifetimes between the lines of forced mathematics
  and creating whole worlds in my backyard.
Places that are more a part of me than any theory.
Now, the empty swing sets creak endlessly as the wind blows each of
  those places away.
There is no play.
The characters are indoors, locked into the dreams of a screen, stuck
  in the land of someone else's invention.
Unable to create their own worlds.

I just keep thinking:
What will become of all those fantastical lands when this *imagined one*
  becomes the only one that there is?   —*Spring 2010*

8. Silence Is Golden

Language is proof that God has a sense of humor.
The way the grunts and hisses have mutated and our brains have
    collected the syllables together is almost as hysterical as the fact
    that words can be beautiful.
I once heard that the most lyrical phrase in the whole English
    language is: *Cellar door.*
Phonetics explains that these are the perfect collection of sounds that
    can be found anywhere.
So much for beautiful.

As a poet, I make a hobby of dissecting words and figuring out what
    they say about our culture.
For example, take the word *freedom*: "free" and "dumb."
Meaning, only the dumb are free.
Like Adam and Eve before they ate from the tree, we believe
    Heaven—perfection—is a return to the blissful ignorance of
    Eden, before our eyes were opened.
When God grew silent we still needed guidance, so we've placed
    leaders over us to rule.
Rule… Rule… Measurements. Rulers.
We need "them" to define us, to give us strict guidelines that we will
    never *measure* up to.
Explain every angle to me, so I can stop thinking.
Free. Dumb.
I want freedom, but not that kind of "freedumb."
Their definition of "Freedom is slavery"; George Orwell got that
    down correctly.
I don't want freedom if it means we must kill everyone to attain it.
When will we stop believing that "War is peace"?
When will we stop bombing our enemies to turn them into friends?
Yes, this type of free is dumb.

Our phrases and sayings illustrate our behavior just as perfectly:
"What do you *do* for a living?"
Meaning, you are only living if you are *doing* something.
The concept of Being was banished with our school systems, which
    encourage empty thinking and a complete lack of enjoying

anything—specifically curiosity and learning.
We praise Alice's Wonderland for its creativity, but only because she
   comes back to the "real" world in the end.
So no, I don't "do" anything for a living.
I *am* living, and what I "do" distracts me from that fact.
Our language grows "Curiouser and curiouser!"

I find it fascinating that there are words I don't know, because this
   proves there is a vast array of concepts, ideas, and things that I
   have never even thought of.
This brings up a remarkable idea—the remark-abled idea—that God
   knows every word in every language and has chosen to remain
   silent.
Funny, ain't it?
There must be something I'm missing.
Maybe I've been analyzing the wrong things:
Focusing too long on "cellar doors," and not enough on what lies
   beyond them.
Stuck in front of closed exits, trying to understand them rather than
   using the doorknob to move on.
Unlike Alice, I do not have the imagination to shrink through the
   keyhole and I have spent my lifetime locked in the rabbit hole.

I've always tried to understand language.
And I *hated* God for Their silence.
I guess it makes sense that They would love me, though I ruin it.
                                                    —*Fall 2010*

9. The Laugh of God

I am a jester of the Universe.
Giggles originate from my being
and erupt from between God's endless lips.

If Metatron is the Voice of God, then
make me The Laugh, because I want to cause
thunder that tickles the Earth on impact.

—Summer 2012

10. "Let There Be Light"

The first picture I ever drew was a heart.
My dad was the chalk and my mom was the paper and together we
    drew innocence.
My origami has since been folded into many shapes and I have
    forgotten the words that were used to whisper planets into
    existence.
Now, the closest I get to such vast creation is gazing at sunrises,
    chanting: "Let there be light."
We can still create days with mere words, if we keep our sense of
    humor about it.

Silence is a language I am no longer fluent in, but I still remember
    how to make hearts beat.
I drag smiles out of frowns, kicking and screaming, because I am
    Love's Jester.
I will play the fool if it will get you to laugh for a moment.

We are infants in Earth's incubator.
Life is a darkroom to develop young souls.
The flashes in our eyes are captured on the film of our hearts.
We are recording devices for the Infinite.

When we are finished here, we will remember the words that
    whispered planets into existence, chanting all together:
    "Let there be light."
The darkness will disappear, revealing the full spectrum of snapshots
    in our hearts.   *—Spring 2011*

11. Faded

When I was a fresh young photograph, not yet a rough sketch fleshed
    out upon the world, I was only potential.
I was pressed out of my creator with no distinguishing features:
A creature that held a world of possibility in my mixture of splotches.
I was born from a flash of firing neurons imprinted upon blankness.
As a young developing design, my dyes aligned:
Blurred edges and frames became clear and fuzziness of fractured
    objects formed into tiny details.
I became a scene that found meaning among the lights and patterns.
I defined myself into the picturesque representation of what I had
    copied.
My portrait became as lucid as the day I was made to reproduce.
Soon after, my picture started to deteriorate.
My Polaroid, polarized:
Darks became lighter. Lights became darker. I became dimmer.
My sleek covered shine flattened into a contorted crumple of
    chemicals and covering.
Silhouetted shadows were all that was portrayed by an aging
    impression of an image, dissolving away.

It seems fitting that we immortalize our lives with something as
    impermanent as we are.
Evanescence is the evolution of this form we take.
We make ourselves complete just in time for our "chrome-osomes"
    to deteriorate.
We live, we create, then we dissipate.
We are perishable and decay renders us all useless eventually.
Life is a single snapshot that begins to disappear soon after it is
    created.
Today's vibrancy fades away tomorrow and eventually all of our
    ephemeral images exist only in the memories of other faded
    impermanence.
Nothing lasts forever.
The ink that produces the pristine-pigments then fragments into
    shades of gray as the days pass.
The chemical reactions that manifest our bodies take away the colors
    in time.

—April 2010

12. White

As long as I can remember, I've sought out new experiences.
I was born with a blank paint-by-number and I wanted to discover
    every color in the cosmos to place into my picture.
Infancy was a yellow frequency: bright as sunbeams and just as
    beautiful;
I often dwelled in the blues and re(a)d between the lines; and with
    these three colors, I thought I understood everything.
But I wasn't satisfied operating at the primary level, so I kept striving
    for colors beyond the basics.
I found secondary, tertiary, and everything in between.
I was a chromatic-consuming machine.
I colored my plain white covering with dyes in any hues I could find.

I wanted to be everything.
But in my search I became stained with labels.
Every degree of taint and tinge saturated within me.
There were beautiful colors:
Star White, Night Black, Silver-Lining Cloud, and Gray Incense.
But I discovered some pigments for which I had no defense—colors
    that I couldn't cover up:
Orange Rage—The color of dried blood when a father beats his son.
Pounding Purple—The pigment of skin after bruises form.
Broken Down Black—The pupils of an eight-year-old child in the
    slums who owns a gun before his first book.
Obscene Green Envy—The reason a beautiful girl is found dead in a
    dumpster.
Brown and Peach—The difference between friendship and death.
Indian Red—An excuse to rob, abuse, and use a whole race of
    people.
Yellow Fear—The real reason for declaring war on the world.
Swollen Belly Blue—A hue of starvation and the hatred that allows it.

In my innocence, I wanted to hold every aspect of the rainbow.
I didn't understand that it would induce an endless pain flow.
My paint-by-number no longer resembled a picture.
Scribbles scratched the surface with violence and the paper flaked
    away in pieces.

The darkness slowly overwhelmed the light and I let myself be
    sucked into it.
Adding more and more and more and more…
Until the lines that defined everything were covered up and my
    picture resembled a jumbled, putrid shade of Shadow Black.

But at the center of the darkest black hole, I found something:
A light so bright it overwhelmed all the other paint.
It was an eraser.
The other side of the pencil.
A force that can conquer even the most terrible of colors.
It was Love.

I now meticulously caress my canvas, turning my paint-by-number
    blank again.
Because there are only two options for those who want everything:
    1. Experience every color in every capacity.
    2. Stay white. Which already contains every chrome, shade,
       pigment, hue, stain, tinge, and tone.

We are born with all the knowledge we will ever know, but the desire
    for more clouds up our masterpieces.

I love what you are doing with your picture, but if you ever want an
    eraser, I'll be happy to lend you mine.
There is an infinite supply where *This* comes from.   —*Spring 2011*

13. When the Skies Turn Red

When I was born, my eyes were connected directly to my heartbeat.
Each time it pulsed I pulled the whole Universe in.
That was until the first time I heard anger.
Hate split apart the Universe I held in each eye as I realized that what
    sprang from nothing also must return there and fear was born
    within me.
But I rewrapped my essence into a gift-paper-covered presence and I
    gave away myself in the most beautiful of methods.
By the time I found words I had already defined reality into what
    people thought of me, with an ego to prove my complacency.
The Universe pulled back from my eyes because I was now defined
    by the words I could speak and the things I could see.

Then school gave me a pencil to permanently prove my reality
    physically.
We memorized periodic tables and were periodically labeled as smart
    for repeating ideas on command, rather than creating our own.
We were taught to forget our heartbeats in favor of the theories
    behind them, because realness is only in what you read.
We were taught to sell our gold-encrusted eyes for the "good life,"
    where we travel blind, walking along roads full of other
    expressionless eyes that confuse our lies with True Beauty.
Evolution robbed us of our vision since we no longer used it.
Now they told us all we needed to know.
In a classroom they told us:
    "The skies are always blue. The skies are always blue. *The skies are*
    always blue! What kind of a fool are you to depict them differently?
    What kind of a fool are you to act irrationally? Distract yourself
    with our numbers and facts. Magic is for the deluded."
Even as they polluted my seas, changed my sunsets from orange to
    green, and replaced my grass with plastic.
A system of eight hours a day beat me down, until I was more lost
    than found.
Feeling around in the dark for a life that lay inside of me.
My daytimes were spent dreaming, believing the skies are always blue.
My dreams were replaced with television scenes:
A sleep that sewed my eye-sockets into sunken, star-struck fantasies.

The roses in my cheeks wilted, yielding only thorns in my eyes.
Smiles once sweet as a chocolate-shop locked together into a rotten-caramel-cemented grimace laced in venom.
My Kundalini snake snapped with poison jaws until my Garden of Eden became a decayed wasteland.
I stayed there for a really long time.
My saving grace is that I don't remember most of that self-serving hell.
You don't remember much when you're a shell.
And time passes quickly when you're not living at all.

But one day the Love-Force entered my Life-Source.
I suddenly saw the words: "Love Movement" staring back at me from bathroom stalls.
Either one person was following me everywhere...
Or there was a radical Revolution of Love happening from the bottom up.
I found myself scrawling the words, "Live, Laugh, Love," on available blank walls and, "Love Matrix," in vacant halls.
I had awoken to a Heaven that was happening all around me that I had been too blind to see.
When it opened my eyes, my own Universe was projected, rather than just reflected.
As I felt my heartbeat for the first time in each moment, I felt the Magic in Life, Love, and Laughing again.
And I dedicated my time to attaining all three, because:
Textbooks don't teach the things worth living for.
And textbooks don't teach the things worth dying for.

So after 22 years of delays, here I am back at stage one, but I'm having a lot more fun in this silly "System".
I'm ready to play without rules or restriction by breaking laws that are riddled in contradiction.
I'm ready for a few more pages in this Fiction.
I'm ready to be my own rhythm.
And you know, this time around...
I'm going to paint those skies red!   —*Winter 2009-10*

14. Paradise Pair of Eyes

There is a dystopian myth that the Earth is in ruins.
In this tall-tale: Humans are a fungus, the culture is growing out of
    control, and the Petri dish planet is running out of room.
But this story was written by a thousand monkeys on typewriters.
It is a Shakespearian story with too much melodrama.
Wake up from the contami*nation* and look past(passed) the
    prophesied future to a world where the whole planet is Heaven,
    where every inch is Eden.
Awakening means seeing the True Beauty and perfection of all
    creatures, even in our ugliest moments.
The bedtime story of our society has lasted for so long that we have
    forgotten the purpose of it.
We have lost the enchantments of infancy.

Have you lost your Paradise Pair of Eyes?
The ones that see rose-colored raindrops when the sky cries?
Have you forgotten Eden? Have you been away *that* long?
There are ancient trees that creek with old wooden bones.
Our first task of morning is to name the new creatures that have
    come into being.
Magic flows in ribbons of dreams, weaving into long hammock naps.
We ride on elephant backs and feast on abundant fruit trees.
There are hidden crevices between rocks where the mountains talk to
    each other.
Their language is so silent that only eternal patience understands it.
Would it make sense for a Perfect God to create a broken planet?
Either the world is cracked, or our lenses are.

Can you see the world as it really is?
Nirvana, Shangri-la, Zion, Utopia—remember it!
Imagine a land where the jungles twist with secrets and the deserts
    are desserts of sugar grains.
In the depths of the Sahara, we are building a giant cupcake
    sandcastle that will never be completed, because the Joy is in the
    building.
Dragons meditate in oases, following their fiery breaths in and out
    with awareness.

Mermaids play music in lagoons on lazy days.
Do you believe in this land I'm describing?
Or is it a far-off fantasy to you?
Imagination is literally a place you can travel to.
Psychology says, "Believing is seeing," so this narrative is as real as
    you think it is.

Remember that each day is a New Awakening.
There is a choir of humble human beings singing of peace every
    morning.
Feast on a fresh-oxygen buffet and dine with the love of friends.
Welcome the Sun's kisses in ecstasy, and re-forge skin cancer into a
    zodiac constellation freckled upon flesh.
Prove to me why you are alive for one more day.
And then rest in the gratitude of that.

Life is creation.
When we stop creating, we die.
When we stop creating new cells, we age and die.
So I am creating a new world with every breath I take, reinventing
    myself every day.
The illusion that the world is dying is very real; suffering is very real.
In some moments that tragedy is winning.
But more often than (k)not, the yarn I am spinning is wrapping itself
    around the hearts of humanity.
I am not alone in this storytelling.
Our Imaginations overlap and invent new planes of being.
But know that if you are not creating your own story, you are living
    in someone else's.

Penicillin is a fungus; it is a disease.
It is also proof that healing can be done exponentially.
It is whichever you choose to believe.
Our lenses frame everything we see, so perhaps it is time to check
    our prescriptions because:
There are more worlds than the one we are experiencing.
There are more worlds than the one we are experiencing.
There are more worlds than the *one* we are experiencing.

—*Winter 2011-12*

15. Vampire R*evo*lution

The *revo*lution is here! I've seen it.
If you haven't, perhaps you're not hanging out with the right people.
Or, more likely, your eyes are just blind to it.
Mutilated vision is an easy prison from our own awareness.
We love the delusions of beauty, fame, power, and money.
We are a society of vampires that can only sleep in a coffin.
Pollution, destruction, and mental decay have laid a fine foundation
    for our graves.
We sleep pleasantly in our cemetery, surrounded by the dying,
    feeding off of the living, bloodsucking traitors that will seduce
    strangers in order to protect our own lives.
A trail of dissolution travels behind us, but we think of ourselves as
    angels bringing about transformation.
We are a world that worships the deceased.
We even make up our departed and offer them eternal life through a
    coffin.
We are mortified by the concept of dying, even as we glorify the
    permanent perfection attained by it.
For a culture that praises an angry God and a resurrected dead savior,
    we still act confused when we mimic their behavior.
Our eternal reign may yet come to an end, as we die just in time to
    see our own funeral.

And yet, I say the *revo*lution is here!
But it's not some mass rebellion.
It's easy to attack our ancestors and forget that the same poison is
    running through our own veins.
This shift is a mental metamorphosis causing an upheaval, but it's *not*
    a mutiny against our leaders.
To rebel against something, we must admit it has power over us.
How do we overthrow an illusion?
The more we attack an idea, the stronger it becomes.
Rather than external wars, this transformation affects mind-states.
It's a new way of living, being, and breathing.
A way of connecting all of our hearts with a string, forming a tapestry
    that blankets all of humanity.
It's a way of existing *between* realities.

This new place is not created through tension and bloodshed.
It is not created by expanding our egos through endless
    consumption.
It is not created with physical ties to this life, or by defining the
    wrong and right way to survive.
It is not created by a God who is less compassionate than we are; in
    fact, that idea is idiotic and irresponsible.

I've seen this transformation:
I've seen vampires dying around me, driving stakes into their own
    hearts, rather than choosing to continue their blood-sucking.
I've seen a mass suicide of the consuming resulting in hearts beating.
I've seen sacrifices of belief systems, the crumbling of prisons, and
    the purging of toxins.
I've seen souls returning and eyes opening.
I've seen coffins burning and crosses melting.
But mostly I've witnessed an awakening of the undead.
As monsters escape from their heads and come to life, they pass back
    through death and inhale a fresh breath of consciousness—taking
    accountability for their actions and becoming true humans.
The new world will not come by force.
It will not be saved by waiting or by recording and reliving the past.
It is something we must find for ourselves.
When we stop feeding off of our lifeless moments, trying to fill our
    veins with the blood of others, with the love of others, only then
    can we live with the luxury of dying—fully appreciating
    everything *because* it is ephemeral.
Only then does it become real.
Only then will we feel life flowing through us:
Revived by the breaths we take.
Excited by the mistakes we make.

You can live as a vampire; it's pretty cool.
But the world is moving on and I'm not sure there's room for the
    bloodsuckers in the new gene pool.
The *revo/ut*ion is happening.
If you haven't seen it, I recommend you get started.
Lest you forfeit your opportunity to experience the world of the
    living.   *—Fall 2010*

16. Tribute to Gandhi
"Be the change you wish to see in the world."

I look around me and I'll tell you what I see:
I see billions caught up in an ego disease, drifting each day further
   away from compassion.
And those who are sleeping are screaming in a way only the
   awakened can hear.
There's fear in their faces, but scream-shattered mirrors keep them
   blind while the virus of self pollutes their minds.

I see people whose insides are peeling:
Petrified paint covers their exteriors, while interiors mold and flake
   off and whole pieces of them simply break off.
They are disintegrating shells whose only souls(soles) are in their
   sneakers.

I see smiles of serpents twisting through breast bones.
I see spirits forgotten in favor of moulds:
Institutions whose goals are contracts and controls, rather than
   acceptance and healing up our holes.
I see people looking for relief as they pray, but if Jesus were alive
   today, he'd be labeled a hippie and his teachings thrown away.
And though I don't know if he's real, I comprehend his concept
   when I look into you:
It's compassion. Passion for the living with a focus on giving.

My friends, as I walk I hear minds talk non-stop, while emotions run
   dry or straight up wither and die.
As our cores corrode, so does our sky.
Landscapes become deserts disease ridden with flies.
This world is a reflection of the one in our eyes and our desires are
   bringing about our demise.
There's a rationing of emotions.
Fixed rational portions when it's convenient.
There's starving, torment, and constant resent.
We're content as we're striving, believing our egos' self-perpetuating
   lying.

But no one can find the dead if they're hiding and at least some are
    screaming and trying, rather than soundlessly accepting their
    dying.
This world makes me speechless, falling apart as we call it "progress."
Our hearts are in distress in the request for understanding.

I see sorrow surrounding our haloes.
I see fear filling our face rolls, dragging them down into wrinkles.
No, I don't know what to say to closed ears.
I don't know how to speak so everyone hears.
But I understand fear, and I understand tears.

I see gods rooted in reality that have forgotten eternity in favor of a
    story.
I see sunflowers attempting to understand the Sun.
Rainbows afraid of the rain.
I see a cyclone made dizzy by its own rotation.
Snow that melts as it hits the ground.
A tree that is dying as it reaches its peak.
But a fire can learn to burn wet logs in the face of extinction, and you
    are as unique as that God you believe in.

Fellow humans, fellow beings, we've been acting as submarines:
Sinking to our lowest point to gain advantages over others.
Believing that conquering will cauterize our own conflictions.
But puddles contain the Universe through reflection.
Branches contain winds by allowing them in.
And boats only move when their sails permit pushing.
Stop dreaming. Focus on living.
Love is like the sky—untouchable.
Yet, it is disintegrating every day.

Regardless, I'll be the change that I wish to see, so that maybe the
    world will become it.
Even just a little bit, because I want to live to sing about it!
Open ears pry eyes open, so listen.
Have some compassion.
Because, my friends: It is *you* that is the change that is ready to
    happen.   —*Winter 2009-10*

17. Still Rocking

The billboard ads promise me dreams:
Artificial one-hit fixes of imitation sunbeams.
While products pull us through this Purgatory, we are stretched
  between lack of sleep and overeating.
Companies are stringing products across our path to prevent us from
  connecting the circuit, while our currency contains everything but
  the current.
But we play their distraction game because once life is perfect, only
  we're to blame for any unhappiness we maintain.

Conniving commercials convince the masses to feed their needs with
  greed and ignorance.
They plant their opinion seeds in your clean-slate cranium vase so
  that when you germinate you create more money-slave seedlings
  buried in the ground.
We lay among the mounds of assembled Frankenstein masses:
A whole race of obese pieces of wasting-away bodies brought to life
  by a television-mind current.
We're rotting as we roll between work and home in order to amass
  more money.
But no amount is enough to make a living since no amount makes up
  for actually living.

In this world, we buy survival in the form of the things we put on
  and we're not worthwhile without a porcelain smile.
We're part of a caste system assigned at birth by an oppressed mess
  of people suppressing themselves!
They have us thinking we aren't worth half that of the jumbo jet set
  of tycoons blazing through the high skies.
With each dollar spent we buy into the idea that "they" are better
  than "us."
You know that everything was once free?
They've just convinced us to pay for it.

But we, individually, are waking up to the fact that life is as free as the
  women we were birthed from and the creations we can become.
Money is only as real as we give it credit to be.

It's a pyramid scheme that has conveniently, deceivingly brainwashed
us into believing in its necessity.
We're prostituting life into the form of an idol we can't eat or drink.
How do we consistently claim to be the "Land of the Free" when
everything here has to be purchased?

Yet, the media will tell you I'm crazy and you shouldn't listen to me.
Because clearly: The more you have and the more you hold, the
smarter you are and the more you know.
My worn-out members represent my lack of wit.
My material absence proves I'm failing the perfectly applicable
system labeled: "The American Dream."
Money-holders are the rightful owners of the entire planet's beings
and I may only live here if I blind my eyes to what I envision and
only repeat their delusion.
I am incapable of understanding my need to be controlled because
my goals of Peace, Love, and Unity represent my ignorance and
lack of understanding.

America, please!
We're above this corporate-cult mind control!
We're building with Love while they're building with hate.
They destroy, while we create.
Let's see how the New World Order operates when the base blocks
stop holding up the top.
Their wars can't be fought if we're all singing rock!
We'll dance in sunbeam rhythms and poetry scenes while they pay
money for imitation dreams.
Instead of angry protests, let's put our passion into creation.
Let's shake the foundations of this nation and be the first generation
to bring about transformation through innovation and inspiration.
Passion is free. I'll say it again: Passion is free!
So burn those bonds of fear.
Because no matter what form their power takes, it can never hold
your soul when it's on fire.   —*Fall 2009*

18. Song of One Tree to Another

A bumble bee hears the hum of her own *buzz* and knows only that.
We are deaf to our own vibrations, lost in the vibrancy of the world.

Plants sing about Life, Death, and the In-Between.
We have forgotten their song in our consumption.

Graze between the planes of Love and Wisdom.
Glide like a swan across the lake's surface.

Reach within and center the mind.
Gently place the flopping fish back in its tank.

Relax into the womb of your own Enlightenment.
The rings of your tree are calling.   *—Winter 2007-08*

19. The Neverland Star

Nightly, instead of drifting off to dreamland, you lock your ankles
    into the mattress.
Shackles secure feet to the ground that you're too afraid to leave,
    because dreams only prophesy things you can never have.
You have run away long enough to know that following shooting
    stars only leads to comets shattered upon the earth.

You think you're muffling the current of sadness radiating from
    inside you, but no silencer could stop the gunshot depression that
    traps you in your head.
For you, midnight mirages manifest into a series of self-hate games.
You play connect-the-dots with the stars, trying to find the way
    everything fits together, but no matter which pattern they form,
    they all say the same thing: "You're not good enough."
So you stay awake igniting the pinpricked sky.
Each light is another lie to keep your eyes open.
Each line you draw in the heavens confines you to yet another box.

My dear, you are beautiful.
You are the Neverland that I can't stand to return home from.
You are the pixie-dust wings I gain by following the second star to
    the right and then straight on until morning.
You are the world of magic tricks.
You are youth and innocence with the smile of crocodiles.
You are the hook pulling me in, the leader of lost boys, and the
    assassin of pirates.
You are timelessness itself.

There is an alarm clock going off inside of you.
It is trying to make you wake up, but like Captain Hook you have
    learned to fear it.
That ticking tock is maddening when it predicts the coming of the
    croc. and you have learned that destroying yourself is the best way
    to escape.
But it only takes one happy thought to fly and I wish you would
    realize that, because Peter Pan only comes in through open
    windows and it is usually when the night is the darkest.

So please, don't close off to the world.
Don't abandon us.
This place has just been taken over by pirates and Peter Pan can
    prove to you that they are much easier to beat than they seem.
So please, don't leave.

You can pursue sadness.
You can forget how to play, you can forget how to crow, and you can
    even grow old—but leave that window open!
In Neverland, our shadows are not glued to our feet.
We are free of them.
We can fly because there is no one Here to tell us that we can't.

Your self-hate has you convinced that things can never change.
The more you lock into that depression, the more trapped you
    become.
The seedy crocodile awaits at the end of the plank, but you can just
    fly over him.
Yet, there is no escape if you do not *believe* there is one.
So think of just one little happy thought.
I promise, you can fly.
But if you jump out that window before you have it, you will only
    destroy yourself.
And the croc. will live on.   *—Fall 2011*

20. One More Day with Jolly Roger

There is a breakdown waiting(weighting) in our hearts for the perfect
  moment to capture us.
It's a pirate ship that drifts below the surface until it sneaks on board.
The other day, this Jolly Roger drifted in front of me and the sturdy
  boat in my chest capsized.
This vessel took anchor in my mind and captured my treasured sanity
  with gunpowder thoughts blasting holes in my well-crafted reality.
These thoughts festered into cankers on the landmass of my lucidity,
  taking over my mind like a flask of rum.
In this moment, I looked to the stars as a compass, shooting cannon-
  blast thoughts into the motionless black flag of the sky:
What if none of this is real?
What if I don't know what to do?
What if I don't know who I am?
What if we are all doomed to die?
What If? What If? What If?
There was no response.
Only the Silence of salty waves seeping into the raw flesh of this
  newly exposed wound.
Only the Silence of a map with no, "You are here," marked on it.
Only the Silent curse of the Universe cast on those who seek its
  plunder.
What If? What If? What If?

Some days I wake up with the Bubonic Plague called Old Age
  poisoning this body and I am tired.
Some days I wake up with the Tuberculosis called Cruelty capturing
  my lungs and cannot breathe.
Some days I wake up with the Scurvy called Selfishness and I don't
  care about anyone but myself.
Some times are hard—almost impossible.
There are days when the Sun only shines because it doesn't know
  what else to do.
There are nights when the Moon doesn't come out at all.
I am a victim to the pirates in myself the same as anyone else.
And sometimes they are winning.
But in these moments, a voice yells from the crow's nest of my mind.

I barely hear it over the lightning crash of my emotions:
"One more day. Just keep breathing."
With my remaining energy, I drag myself out of bed and go swab the
    decks of my hull until I have gained control over the sea monsters
    of Davy Jones' Locker that are attacking my vessel from below.
When it feels like the heavens have abandoned me, lost at sea, I take
    a deep breath and look to the Sun and say:
"If you can rise every day and shine with such brightness, so can I."
"If you can burn for so long without burning out, so can I."
"If you can carry such Light in your eyes, so can I."
It is from this that I have acquired my sworn occupation of Soul
    Brightener.
This job is not work, but it is exhausting.
Yet, I wake every day and do it anyway because:
Perhaps we will find peace today.
Perhaps the wars will end and we will feel compassion today.
Perhaps we will embrace our neighbors and drop the daggers that
    reside in our eyes today.
Perhaps we will care more about our crews and less about what is in
    our holds today.
Perhaps the black pirate flags make more sense than all the colors
    that divide us.
Perhaps we will have the chance to love a little longer…
Perhaps. Perhaps. Perhaps.
What If? What If? What If?

When I finally run out of gunpowder, I relax my attack and rephrase
    my questions; but this time, I pick up my anchor and surrender to
    the ocean currents.
And this time, the Silence Replies:

It is the perfect answer.
It stings like peroxide poured straight into the vena cava of my heart.
It fizzles and bubbles the infection that lies there:
What If? What If? What Iffffffffffffffff————------
It burns away the rotted flesh that lies within the crevices of my
    Inner Thunder Maker.
The answer hurts as much as it heals.

There are moments in life that steal our sanity.
I cannot give you the answers that will patch up those cannon blasts.
I cannot take away the Dark Nights of the Soul, nor would I wish to.
There are moments when Jolly Roger casts his shadow upon your
    heart.
He may leave you vacant and shipwrecked on an abandoned isle, but
    do not fear.
You are the captain of a vessel that cannot be stolen.
Collect your strength, assemble your ship, find your compass.
And have a little faith that you will find a way through the Bermuda
    Triangle—where no pirates dare follow you.   *—Summer 2012*

21. Stardust

Sex is like stardust drifting from the sky onto a pathological planet
that insists on bathing in apathy.
It is little flickers of the Real onto a tub filled with fallacy, emptiness,
and loss.
The no-substance-required drug that God imbedded within our skin.
Active and powerful, overwhelming and enjoyable, consuming and
full.
It is a flower that blooms in the mind with white flashes and opium-
poppy-seed dreams, with vines that wrap from curled toes
through butterfly stomachs to entwined minds.
It causes energies to mix into fantastic new flavors on soul-tongues
that gleefully *slurp* up new frequencies of silent-note screams.
As limbs wrap around limbs and bodies become shooting stars,
supernovas drift from the skies into the eyes of star-crossed
lovers.
Lovers who quickly forget what planets are and get lost in
earthquake-shattering quivers.

Sex is not simply procreation of post-pubescent primates, going
through motions marked by ancient-instinct desires, simply to
continue the species.
It is not merely movements meant to whittle away at life's repetitive
moments.

Sex is when the mind gets lost in mazes that only infuriate you as you
travel forward.
It is serpentine secrets whispered in your ear that dare you to eat the
apple and taste what it's like to be a god, flavoring each bite with
what's it's like to feel good for once.
It fills hearts with gasoline while holding a match just close enough to
tempt an explosion.
It's a drum line that pulses in booming, megaphone-enhanced, stereo
sound as strings play symphonies on your cerebellum.

How dare anyone say sex is sinful.

As beads of sweat become raindrops on the heart, it opens the
floodgates of the soul, reducing everything to its basic elements
and allowing you to see someone as their simplified self, no
complications required.
Sex allows Heaven to stare back at you through a pair of post-
ecstasy-high eyes.
It allows you to get lost on another level of existence with a person
and happily drift with no path back.
It allows you to dance among angels with your lover in rapture and
capture reality between bed sheets.

Sex is a near-life experience.

It causes the stardust we are created from to crumble to the ground
as we awaken into a post-big-bang Universe composed of
carefully constructed chaos.
Society couldn't strip the surrealism from the action so they declared
it sinful.
Hoping to take away your humanness and replace you with an
emotionless, working, robot drone-slave living in the dark.

But they forgot that sex is like stardust.
Each time two lovers meet in the back alleys of society and fuck away
all the bullshit that feeds our everyday existence, a new star is
created in the Universe.
Let's all create new stars in the Universe and form whole galaxies
until the sky fills with great beacons of light and every living
person can only gasp at the awesome array of Love on the
horizon.
Because sex is what made each one of us; it is the *only* life-bringer.
It makes no difference what form it takes or how you choose to do it;
sex brings passion to a sometimes apathetic existence.

No matter what Hollywood turns it into or the broken world believes
it to be:
Sex is a beautiful, celestial miracle.   —*Spring 2009*

22. All the Way to the Sun

A butterfly's wings whip across my eyes,
causing the lovely Aphrodite to
burst from the foam chrysalis in my heart.

The Sun lowers from the sky in a blaze,
and sets upon the mountains of my chest,
cauterizing my tongue on the way down.

This mysterious little butterfly
has tapped my soul with a hammer and nail
so gently it barely nicked the surface.

But the sore has become infected and
I want nothing more than to drive the nail
deeper until my heart has swallowed it.

Love, I would have escaped up the vast steps
of the Giant Lotus Flower by now.
But I'll wait on this side of paradise:

'Til we both grow all the way to the Sun.
                            —*Winter 2008-09*

23. Blackbird

For those who fight for the freedom to love.
Italics indicate lyrics from "Blackbird" by The Beatles.

Two eyes on a face; one looks to the other and sees it as different:
"We are so opposite. I'm on the left; you are on the right. We have
    nothing in common."
"'Tis true," says the right, "My eye(I) is better than yours."

The Sun looks to the Moon:
"You steal my light. I will fight you to get it back."
The Moon replies, "What's yours is now mine. One sun's trash is
    another moon's treasure."
Their very reflections separate them.

Boys on the left. Girls on the right.
Girls play with dolls. Boys play with guns.
Girls have pink. Boys have blue.
The planet is divided in two nations:
Male and Female.
The right eye versus the left.
The Sun versus the Moon.
Gender permits a war to exist in plain view, but we don't see our
    prejudice because it is so normal for us.
The age-old scheme of "Divide and Conquer" is in full effect.
"It's a girl!" "Congratulations on your baby boy."
It is a label that dictates the rest of our lives.
Divide and Conquer.
Tell me, why aren't there separate bathrooms for blondes and
    brunettes?
Why isn't eye color asked on standardized tests?
Gender as a measure for what a person is capable of.
Divide and Conquer.

When I was five, my best friend was a little boy:
Blonde hair, blue eyes, fair skinned, and enormous white wings.
Mockingbirds ripped my vibrant dove from me:
"Boys don't play with girls."

Divide and Conquer.
I remember his white flag of surrender, crafted from his severed right
    wing, bleeding as he tucked his soiled tail feathers between his
    legs and disappeared.
For the next eight years, I could only watch the shadow of my
    beloved dove from afar.

"Blackbird singing in the dead of night,
take these broken wings and learn to fly..."

It was not until we were thirteen that we could be friends again.
Then it was acceptable for boys and girls to be together.

"Blackbird singing in the dead of night,
take these sunken eyes and learn to see."

Eventually we saw the hypocrisy in it all.
Gender was but a label that cut apart our friendship.

"All your life, you were only waiting
for this moment to be free."

Since then, I've abandoned sexual stereotyping and I only see people.
This practice has gained me another great label: "Bisexual."
The governed are truly dominated when they self-enforce the rules
    they are given.
The Pharaoh maintained control in Egypt by getting the slaves to
    fight amongst themselves:
Divide and Conquer.
Gender is the real root of our separation, wars, battles, religion,
    power, greed.
And we sustain it.

I am not "bi" and this is not a "coming-out poem."
I do not fight or desire both teams.
I am at peace with both.
There is a lot more to a person than what does or does not hang
    between their legs.
We all have eyes, lips, brains, and skin.

We are all human.
Gender is a rusted cage that locks away the pearls of the soul.
It kills potential.
There is a lustrous spark that happens in someone's eyes when they
    are awake.
I fall in love with that.
Fixating on sex seems prehistoric.
Just knock me over the head with a club and drag me back to your
    cave, my big strong man.
No, I form bonds with every person I meet, not just fifty-percent of
    them.
I love profoundly, whether or not it leads to touching.
I am more impressed with the content of your character than the
    formations of your skin.

"Blackbird fly, into the light
of the dark black night."

The battle only continues if we pick a side.
It is only when there is no difference between us that the ivory flag of
    peace prevails.

The right eye looks upon the left:
"You are so beautiful. I wish I could be more like you."
To which the left replies, "You are. You are just *right*."

The Sun looks upon the Moon:
"You are so brilliant; you truly make the light Divine."
The Moon replies, "It is our light. I am not sure when 'mine'
    becomes 'yours.' We are brilliant together. Not one without the
    other."
                                                                  —*Fall 2011*

24. War Flowers

War is always glorified in the media.

The way movies twist romance into war scenes is sickening.

It's almost as if they are saying that war actually breeds love.

When I saw the movie *Pearl Harbor*, I found an extreme irony in the fact that the atomic bomb was totally left out of that picture.

We ignore the mushroom-cloud catastrophes that have been planted in our world-garden, but there is no way to forget the fatal fungus fumes that have infected our planet.

I only hope we have not acquired a taste for the spores in our ever-growing appetite.

Luckily for our sanity, our memory groves only stretch far enough to get us what we want, and war is a concept forgotten as soon as it is vomited verbatim onto multiple-choice bubbles.

But to those who think war is romantic, please go visit the soldiers returning in a casket.

Their flag-draped shells hide the bodies beneath a symbol of freedom so that we won't see them.

We plant these expired souls in the ground, hoping that they will grow into half the beings they once were.

Their bloodshed is covered with a million red-petal "reasons" and sweetened with the perfume of ignorance.

But nothing quite covers the sickening stench of foul play, and it only takes a glance to see that we are sowing dead seeds in the ground.

Our cemeteries are sprouting into an endless forest of tombstones that will never bear fruit.

But what are a few deaths in a world of billions?

Yet, our returning dead trees are the lucky ones.

Our veterans return to us twisted and rotting.

Each ring formed after combat is sickly thin and broken.

War is a storm that blows our young saplings over.

Healthy humans must be broken before they can kill each other, and from that point on they never truly recover.

What are we saying by recreating war stories and watching them for entertainment?

It's only a step away from the Roman Coliseum, where people also
  died for their freedom.
When has killing ever brought peace?
Why have we never attempted a complete ceasefire?
If a better world is our goal, there are a million other answers.
For example: the best use of the 700-billion-dollar "Defense Budget,"
  would be to feed, clothe, and shelter the world, because happy
  people don't destroy each other.

I'm tired of seeing sawed-off tree-stumps surrounded in rotten fruit.
I want a rainforest of human beings with green leaves, stretching
  their arms into endless canopies of poetry.
I want thriving lives with deep roots that pump out oxygen every
  time they bat their eyelashes.
I'm not asking for some unattainable Utopia; I just want to stop
  fighting.
I want to stop glorifying death as a way to rationalize our losses.
Each life taken is a sharp thorn in my chest.
Our idealistic "reasons" are a ferocious fang in my heart.
I feel paralyzed with the venom that is seeping through our system.
I'm sick from listening to the word-tricks of serpents with ulterior
  motives.
How are we still failing to see that the "Kill You Before You Kill
  Me" mentality isn't working?
We've tried it. We've been trying it.
Why are we so afraid to try something else?
You can protect yourself by killing everyone else, but the price of
  your "safety" is a fate I don't envy.
We only get a short time here, and anything we accomplish will mean
  little in 50 years.
But if you take a life, it is one of the only acts you can't take back.
And no matter what your "reason" was, no matter how good your
  intensions seem:
That species of flower, that version of a person is now extinct
  forever.
And nothing you will ever create in your entire life can ever live up to
  the creation you destroyed.   —*Spring 2011*

25. Pick It. Keep It. Own It.

Some people make it strikingly easy to see God in their eyes.
Their pores scream Freedom, even when their pages crumple and
    their skin wears thin.
I once asked a beautiful old man how he stayed so happy as age was
    robbing him of vitality.
He responded, "Because my life is perfect and I have never suffered.
    Or I have suffered enough to overcome it. You pick. And when
    you do, keep it. Own it."
Since then, I've shifted my vision and I live in an enchanted forest of
    Imagination where each person I meet is a shaman or magician.
I don't own every rose in this forest.
It is enough to preserve their Beauty in memory.
To own a rose is fleeting and saddening.
It disintegrates the minute you pick it, keep it, own it.
And yet, maybe that's what makes them so desirable:
The slow death that awaits something so beautiful.
Admit it: We're all that evil sometimes.
So, be the best you can. Be alive.
Because that's the least sinful thing I can think of.
If we must trample a few flowers to understand destruction, it's
    worth it... If we learn from it.
There is purpose in the breakdown if it breaks down the stagnant.
The mightiest forest is burned down to make room for new roses.
Unfortunately, we cannot own the world.
If we could, we would see that we don't want to.
To own the world is fleeting and saddening.
It disintegrates the minute you pick it, keep it, own it.
But maybe that's what makes it so desirable:
The slow death that awaits something so beautiful.
I have not perfected the art of living any more than a painter can
    perfect the art of creation, but I know that one day, you will
    discover yourself as a sunflower in a field.
When you do: pick it, keep it, own it.
To live is fleeting and saddening.
Yet, maybe that's what makes it so desirable.
We are all experiencing a slow death that awaits everything so
    beautiful.   —*Spring 2011*

26. Rose

A beautiful rose
blooms in a field because it
is there to bloom in.

—Winter 2007-08

27. Existence

There's the rhythm of a drum inside these lines, full of folded note
    cards with poetic rhymes and I just keep beating, pulsing in time
    to a *thump thump thump* that mimics the Divine.
The inspired are confusing to the lost and the silenced, while fire
    spreads quickly to the rising defiant.
Is having everything the path to paradise?
Or does it lead to an empty string of sidewalks connecting our
    chatterbox minds to the same old repetitive designs of the same
    old horizon lines?
Can we really be content in the purity of perfection?
Or will the passion-less, unflawed features seem empty and inhuman?
We choose the realities of our own tapping toes that meanwhile trap
    us to the paths we travel.
We hide love behind the dreams of masochistic desires that force us
    to forget our purpose.
But don't beat yourself up too badly: We are only as weak as the God
    that is Everything and Nothing.

Rocking and relaxing from moment to moment, we coax the world
    into spinning and spinning as we keep singing our way through to
    gentle expression.
Inspiration is the tempest of Truth that answers our lost egos.
To understand you, is to understand me, and only then can "We" be.
For a hug is the answer to all of life's problems, a kiss makes the
    world explode, and sex is ethereal.
There's no difference between the hum of the wind and the breath of
    a lover, when they make you smile and feel wholly worthwhile.
As our hearts keep beating and we're breathing as one, that's all that's
    required of our little toy drum.
It's the *tap tap tap* as we dance along, finding the point of this journey.

So remember: You are every bit of the beat in your heart.
You are every bit of the air you breathe.
And that feeling of the Divine?
That's the rhythmic pounding of possibility that latches on,
    connecting you to the un-ignorable chorus line moving in time.
This is Existence.   *—Winter 2008-09*

28. Visions of Venus

Our energy glows in a purple and gold halo around us.
There's peace in my being, but my eyes look more like a fire pleading
    for oxygen—eager and thirsty.
My heart threads in and out of my chest, attempting to climb into
    your body.
If only for a moment, I want to feel the pulse of your marrow in my
    fingertips and catch glimpses of the pictures in your mind.
It's the evanescence of your presence that makes this moment more
    precious.
I wish to scratch nails on the surface of your shoulder blades, and
    trace riddles on your spine to define reality on the contradictions
    that lie there.
Grasping onto the infinite possibilities of a daydream.

What is reality but a fantasy brought to life?
What is sight but an optic nerve battling against the light?
What is passion but a delusion made authentic?
You are a hallucination that borderlines between certainty and
    confusion—a vision that I imagined while trapped in a mirage.
Your image is that of a contorted nightmare that I don't want to
    wake up from.
I've become spellbound from your ensnaring entrapments, enchanted
    by the tricks that are meant to draw me in.
Like an insect aroused by the nectar of a Venus Fly Trap, I can't
    resist against the teeth that would lash into me.
Bite down on my flesh and I'll press my skin to yours—devoured by
    the hypnotic powers of your eyes.
As light blurs our seduction into the realm of the imagination, our
    fire-lit fingers spark embers upon luminous skin, reflecting the
    transparency of our bodies as our spirits glimmer from within
    them.
Hand-stoked passion lingers on the surface in a phantom caress—not
    quite real, but overwhelming nonetheless.

Tantalizing and intoxicating, your lips are an aphrodisiac that I want
    to taste between breaths.
Your skin is a love potion I want to consume continuously.

Your kisses are a blazing inferno scorching against a blizzard—a
 combustion of cool crisp contours and burning desires.
I want to whisper oxygen into the flames of your soul and feed the
 urges that lie there with words that can capture the hunger.
I crave the searing burns that occur when your tongue ignites my
 neckline.
It brings this phantasmal paradise to life, so that I can believe the
 dream a little longer.

Your eyes remind me of an evil genie, infinite possibilities—scary,
 but the rewards far outweigh the danger.
Even if your manifestation is an illusion, I'd risk the imprisonment of
 insanity just to dance in between the concepts of truth and fallacy
 with you.
The semblance of your appearance is reality enough for me to risk
 dreaming, but I'd risk deceiving the gods themselves for the
 charred skin I receive from your flaming embrace.

I am a sorcerer that longs to play with your fire—to feel warmth
 between fingertips and drift amidst visions.
You are a figment fabricated within a fantasy—a figure formed with
 flickering dreams.
It is impossible to follow your light, but believing doesn't require
 eyes, and I can feel your breath in everything.

You are intangible, impossible; a reality that only exists when I'm not
 looking; an insanity that only persists when I'm fighting against
 reality.
Yet, I question my eyes, trusting in lies, because even if you are only
 half of the truth, it's a half I wouldn't have without you, and
 therefore:
It is worth all of the madness.   *—Fall 2010*

29. Sacred Mothers

I. Gaia

My vagina is a garden, where the air is moist in humidity and un-
catchable birds of paradise fly through the canopies.

My vagina is an exotic landscape where tropical flowers bloom in
distilled Beauty.

My vagina is the Mariana Trench with unknowable secrets.

It's a crystal cave, a lightning storm, the serene peak of Mount
Everest.

My vagina is a beautiful Egyptian desert oasis flowing in abundance.

When he took me, he did not believe in the Beauty of an unpicked
rose.

He only saw something he wanted and planted his flag in the soil of
my sacred land.

He did not understand the Native American way of worshipping
what is not yours.

He did not understand that some things are priceless.

Some things are Holy.

"Tread lightly on your mother's breast," his snide eyes cracked with
laughter.

He is a mother fucker and proud of it.

To him, my vagina is an oil field to be sucked and fucked dry, a
flower petal to be drained of its essence and worn as his perfume,
a servant that bends to the whims of her master and stands in
shackles with no will of her own.

To him, my vagina is under his superior power to be commanded
and controlled.

But to those who would hold me back, I have but one thing to say:

I AM GAIA! The great womb of the world.

I birthed every one of you.

I am the Mother of your Mother's Mother's Mother's Mother's
Mother's Mother's … Mother.

Creator of all you see.

Your lands are *my lands* from sea to shining sea.

You play your little war games, but my Warmth is the spark in your
chest.

I am the only thing dividing you from the frozen VOID of space.
You are not a mistake; I have no plans to abort you.
I do not give up on my children before they have a chance at Life.
I will not give up on you.
Drain the milk from my breast; I will nurture you.
Defile my sacred flower; I will nurture you.
Take my thighs around your hips and kiss me deeply, penetrate my
    darkest regions with your insanity, rape me daily; I will nurture
    you!
They call me Goddess, Mother Earth, Sacred Mother.
I am not at your level; I do not hold grudges.
I forgive the moment your knives slice open my flesh.
I accept the demons you plant in my soil with smiles.
I love you. I always have. I always will.
Take me. Make me. I am yours.
                                                    —*Summer 2012*

II. Yggdrasil

Call me Yggdrasil.
I was once the great Nordic tree of legends, holding the worlds
    together, an old woman with the Wrinkles of Time pressed into
    papier-mâché branches.
My back creaks in old redwoods and my soul is the burning core of
    volcanoes.
I have dipped my toes in Pompeii's ashes and drank the teardrop
    rains of Atlantis.
I am the mother of the whole forest.
I was once considered the very source of Life itself.

Long ago, Man placed a crown of laurel branches around my
    outstretched finger, promising to love me forever.
I hold this ring so deeply that it etches itself on my trunk every year.
But as time passes, Man becomes less and less impressed with me.
He hates the maple syrup of my breast, but siphons it away like a
    hooker's cheap gift.
He has morphed into the wyrm-dragon Niohagger, living at my
    roots—a great serpent tearing away my flesh, even while I house
    and protect him.

In Man's conquest of Nature, it would never do to have a mere tree,
an old woman, supporting his burdens.
So in a final act of betrayal: He gave my job to Atlas.
Can you imagine a mere human holding the world on his shoulders?
It is no wonder Gaia rocks back and forth in space—lost and alone.

I have surrendered my place in the heavens, but my branches still
reach through to Valhalla; my hands are wrinkled lotus flowers;
and my heart still weaves the cradle of existence together.
Whole forests are born from my thighs, but Man has aborted them,
leaving my woodlands littered in dead piles of amputated stumps.
I have considered returning with a vengeance, covering Gaia's flesh
with Venus Fly Traps that feast on sin.
I've considered creating a weed that feeds on greed.
I've considered twisting the Sun's rays into toxins that burn those
who *act* as vampires.

But in these moments, our wedding vows come back to me.
I admit: I have considered turning on you.
But in true feminine power, I can only turn *from* you:
Turning a blind eye and turning the other cheek.   *—Summer 2012*

30. For Sale

For those who suffer from the sex-slave industry.
Let us find a resolution that frees everyone. So mote it be.

Her room smells of incense and stale sheets, a stench that sticks in
her nostrils as a constant reminder that she is a slave.

The hummingbird hum of cars passes by outside her window, but
she stares at blank walls bouncing back white noise only
perceivable in dreams.

Eyes pried awake, she traces ceiling ridges, falling into their contours,
doorways into the Land of Shadows where hope is the single
most mysterious thing she has never seen.

Eyes once ignited in kerosene appear as a distant flickering
lighthouse, barely distinguishable from illusion.

Her arms form bandages around her frail body, holding her pale
china pieces in place so they don't disintegrate.

The room's stillness reveals only the mumbling swamp cooler—a
monster destroying what's left of the warmth in her life.

She shivers beneath the sheets, attempting to blanket her body with
their comfort.

Each one covers another layer of self-hatred and blame that she's
hidden beneath, but their warmth is worth the weight they hold
her down with.

Slow breaths drift along her skin as she pulls into herself.

A lifetime of struggle has conditioned her, positioned her awareness
outside of her body.

She cannot feel the heat of her own heart, though its beating is the
only thing still connecting her to reality.

Beating is the only thing connecting her to reality.

She craves the beatings because it is the only thing still connecting
her to reality.

It throbs consistently—brings consistency—pulsing heavily, steadily,
as it breathes in the silence and converts it to sweat beads.

Her hands convulse inward, grinding nails in to skin and gripping
sheets between fingers.

She pulls at the fabric forming a refuge around her, forcing her soul
to stay inside rather than run to the rumbling cars outside.

She thinks of hummingbirds… and wonders how a heart could beat
so fast and still last through the night.

She remembers when she used to fight back.

Though it is barely a memory, it is one that she could never forget.

She remembers the repercussions—the percussions of fists pressed
against cheekbones.

Oh, she remembers the repercussions.

Eyes glaze over as she falls deeper into the mattress; she can barely
distinguish its ridges and folds from her own contours.

She thinks of hummingbirds and wonders how they learn to fly so
fast, the contrast between those fleeting wind speeds and
stopping seems impossible.

If only she could get her wings to fly swiftly enough to free her.

She stares at blank walls that bounce back white noise once believed
to be only perceivable in dreams, but she hears their emptiness
like screams of an un-dialed radio on full volume.

Projected nothingness reverberates her bones against each other as
knees knock together, breaking the blood vessels of her ridges
and contours.

She can barely distinguish pain from pleasure and craves the
distraction of bruises because they draw her attention from the
cold.

There are never enough blankets to warm her.

Others' body heat brings sweat, but only freezes her core.

Breaths bypass her skin and sink directly into her marrow, flowing
straight into her steady heartbeat.

Ironically, breath has become her mortal enemy.

She thinks of hummingbirds: With feathers to cover their flesh, they
would never be against a breeze to lift them up.

She thinks of hummingbirds: Sampling sweet nectar in place of
charcoal shakes she ingests forcefully.

She thinks of hummingbirds: Her only connection to the world that
lies outside, the only thing keeping her alive inside a slowly
disintegrating body.

She thinks of hummingbirds…

Then returns to white walls projecting static only perceivable in
dreams.   —*Spring 2010*

31. Restricting Words

You're the type of person romance was invented for.
The type that old poetry adored.
The world spins to your rhythms and yields to your whims, whether
    or not you ask it to.
And though I sometimes have to search to see your energy, I know
    that your frailties are some of your greater qualities.
But I wish you'd smile again. With real whole smiles, not pieces.
Not practiced reactions to roll into face creases.
Smiles that could convert whole countries to capitalism.
That would make you the perfect politician.
The ones that could convince Jesus to sin.
Smiles that sing like songbirds in Spring, heard even by a deaf world.
The day we met, you liquefied my soul with those smiles and blew
    bubbles into my heart-cup with kisses.
I was convinced that even in a world of miracles, your existence was
    still impossible.
I was convinced of magic again.
I was convinced my life was a fiction, because that's the only place
    heroes appear in.
I was overwhelmed within, by a love I wasn't ready to be in, by a
    fullness I couldn't contain.
But those smiles slowly faded away back into my daydreams and I
    found that I was in love with a picture sucked of its meaning.
As you lost yourself, I lost you too.
I hope someday love is something you can be, breathe, and believe in
    with kisses that contain as much as the ones you receive, and I
    hope someday you'll understand that even a quarter moon still
    brightens the night sky.
It's no wonder why you stay at less than full light: Full brilliance
    would overwhelm every other radiance.
I miss those magnificent moonbeams, but I thank Life for your
    imperfections; otherwise I'd be *totally* lost in your essence, instead
    of just *mostly*.
When your journey is ready to move on, I'll be waiting for those
    smiles over the next horizon.
Where music notes make up the steps, so that as you walk, your
    songs play in full illumination.   —*Winter 2009-10*

32. One Ocean

Sometimes I look at the sky and the stars flirt back at me.
In those moments they remind me of you.
Your skin is a million luminous stars that I wish to be upon.
I long to lay my breasts against your back and wrap around you like
the Moon wraps around the Earth, feeling your dense core pulling
me ever closer to your gravity.
Nights when dreams drag me into the heavens, I find myself
caressing your flesh in the hopes that your stardust will entwine
with mine.
When you press into me, the soft light shining from between your
skin cells forms into a whole galaxy, and I am transported to a
universe that doesn't really exist, grinding lightning kisses into
Moon-lit lips.
My fingers sail along the meridian of your backbone as I trace the
constellations in your eyes.
Amidst the fusion, subconscious screams soak our bodies in the
white-hot light of two atoms merging, the audible silence of
breaths expiring before they are even spent.
Eyes press back closed in moans that barely escape, reshaping our
black holes and supernovas together back into thunder.

I wonder, when I speak in endless similes, is it any less powerful to
just say: "I want you"?
I want to feel you inside as my chakras ignite—like a bright rainbow
sparkler, slowly burning embers along the line of my backbone.
I desire the firework finale on the Fourth of July, the one that was
worth fighting for.
I seek shrieking explosions of bottle rockets cracking against an
endless sky of the Universe that resides inside of me.
I want to set fire to dynamite doused in kerosene, throw it into a
building, and enjoy the repercussions of a burst, followed in
collapse.
I want to make light brighter than the stars, brighter than either of
ours on their own.
I want to make passion into something tangible, physical.
I want to feel the impossible.

I want to prove that stars aren't real because the gravity we propel
  outward is more powerful than all of them.
I want the stars to wish upon us.
I want comets that never fade.
I want fireworks to give up because they couldn't possibly compete
  with us.
I'm talking sex without "sexpectations."
I'm talking about creating something.
I want to put the "moment" back in momentum.
I want a force that can't be contained.
I want your best and I want your worst and I want it so bad it hurts
  you.
I want the waters of the sky to stop fighting against the ocean.
I want to see them unified together, as one.
I want all of matter to implode just so I can show you what I'm
  feeling and know that you understand it.
If everything is energy, I want to short-circuit the entire cosmos with
  our endless electricity.

You are a universe that I want to explore to the ends.
I want to understand God in the palm of your hand.
I want to create something so incredible that it must be finite.
I want to spend time fighting for something that has to die.
I want to create and destroy all of existence in a moment, and have
  nothing to show for it.
And after the exhaustion sets in, I want to do it all over again.
Some call sex a sin and with you it is.
Because by the time we're done, I would erase a million planes of
  reality, just for the *memories* of those places we've been.

—*Fall 2010*

33. BBQ Heart

Electricity pulses through my veins.
My soul feels like a barbequed hot dog.

But once cooked, my heart is ready to be
snatched and eaten by the delightful Chef.

—Winter 2005-06

34. Emerald Lighthouse

I have cried enough for the human condition to force Lucifer to
    question original sin.
My heart has a hole wider than the eye of a needle and camels race in
    by the thousands.
How come we forget our hearts, when we can always feel them
    moving?
Is it so much easier to beat the world around us than feel the beat
    within us?
When did our heart-songs become a requiem?

Human suffering is a battleship dodging devastation as meteorites
    rain down in battalions.
All the masons in the world cannot create a lighthouse that
    illuminates brighter than we do, but hate shatters the lens that
    projects that light outward.
Yet salt heals, so I collect liquid sorrow in tear ducts, store them in
    my chest's aquifer, and use them to irrigate the world's droughts.
My gypsy tears trickle inward until my heart is a well of tormented
    droplets collected one by one from your seas and ready to quench
    your thirst.
But I have not come to steal your oceans.
I am here to pump them out of you like a medic, preventing you
    from choking on your own agony.
Give me the geyser of your anguish and I will hold it as dear as the
    Fountain of Life.
Water conducts electricity, so surrender your sadness.
I will use it to energize my body into a Love Battery until I am a
    superconductor of the Universal Concert.

There is an emerald tuning fork in our chests called Unconditional
    Love.
We are electrical currents channeled into light.
When we project it outward, we become a force of Enlightenment.
When we hoard it within, we become electric chairs.
Give me your teardrops, and I will broadcast Eternal Love, becoming
    an auditory lighthouse to guide wayward travelers back home.

I am not here to save anyone.

Yet, it is the hardest thing I have ever had to do: to sit by and watch the world drown itself.

But how else will we learn?

If people want to take their boats to the End of the World, they might sail off the edge.

We cannot steer the ships of the lost, only act as a lighthouse to bring them home.

We cannot stop the meteors from raining down, only provide enough light to avoid them.   *—February 2013*

35. Circus Swimming Pool

The tears you don't cry could create beautiful lullabies as they slide
  down soft skin and dissolve your face-covered lies.
But you hold back, fold back within yourself, and the sadness gets
  trapped in a mental heart-attack of spasms and releases.
Pushing those eye drops deeper into distillation in the creation of a
  direct depression line that will last a lifetime.
Your inner child is held inside, while you wave wands to distract.
Your magic is an act to tie up tears inside while you drown in your
  own eyes, but you're only fooling yourself with the tricks you try.
I can't sit by, embracing lies, but I can't help if you don't ask.
Masks are for stage-side tricks and fear is for back-alley addicts, but
  you bask in a mix of the two, practicing ignorance of emotions
  and ignoring the monsoon happening in your head.
You try to get through it alone, but you think water-works don't
  work, so puddles of the eyes become burst lead-pipe flood-zones
  in your heart.

Meanwhile: I don't know what to say.
I don't know how to play in circus-fire-ring barriers, though I would
  willingly take cosmic burns just to see your brightest smile light
  up in sun-fire circle rays.
But I don't know what to say.
I don't know how to play in the tear-filled waters deeper than ocean
  trenches, surrounded in caged fences with shackles on my feet,
  beaten from lapping waves, mind-slave to boiling temperature
  heat as salt water burns my throat!
I can only write words in stretched out poetic stanza strings and sing
  broken music refrains in the attempt to release you from your
  circus act:
The trapeze artist, tightrope walker, unhappiness stalker, angry-
  elephant stomper, creepy-music-box projector, fearful-fake
  clown-dance, big-top-circus-ring show you project around
  yourself.

I may not know what to say.
I may not know how to play by the rules you've come up with today.
I don't know how to pull the drain plug to your eyes' murky waters.

But a hug takes no words, crying requires no coaches, and talking is
    free.
I hope, eventually, when you're tired of drowning and done with the
    routine, you'll think about asking for help.
I know you could cry on your own, but you don't have to cry alone:
    There's always a friend to help you.
You hold all vulnerable emotions inside, and I honestly don't know
    why.
Because each tear you don't cry could create beautiful lullabies as
    they slide down soft skin and dissolve your face-covered lies.

—June 2009

36. Band-Aid

I don't want to swim
in the same pool as
a pus-soaked band-aid.

So I swim to the
opposite side and
pretend it's not there.

—Fall 2005

37. Thank You
A Prayer of Gratitude

Thank You for oxygen.
It is a battery that keeps me energized
and fuels every step of my vast journey.

Thank You for this body.
It is a massive Pinocchio puppet that explains Truth to me,
a life-sized doll at my command.

Thank You for food.
A complex orchestra brings it to me
and I adore the symphony of flavors in each mouthful.

Thank You for my home.
I am a turtle with a soft center and my hermit cave
offers cool sanctuary from the burning world.

Thank You for health.
I experience existence through the lens of this body
and when I feel good it is easy to see how beautiful Life *is*.

Thank You for family—both chosen and given.
I meet You through my fellow man
and these beautiful souls make it easy to understand Divinity.

Thank You for tears.
Each one holds the Universe,
sparkling straight from the black hole in my core.

Thank You for smiles.
They are a Truth that everyone forgets to mention.
Perhaps they are too sacred for words to risk the corruption.

Thank You for laughter.
Sometimes I want to be angry,
but happiness stabs me in the chest and I die in a puddle of giggles.

Thank You for Love.
Thank You for Love.
Thank You for Love.

Thank You for Life.
It is beyond me and all I can do is promise to show up every day,
and play as nicely as I can with the other children.

Thank You for Death.
It is the Greatest Mystery of this place,
and mystery is one of my favorite things.

Thank You for suffering.
The lessons are hard to learn,
but I grow like a desert rose upon a prickly cactus.

Thank You for the Moon.
When I look up at the beams
they lay across my heart like a band-aid.

Thank You for the Sun.
I awoke this morning to the illumination of His infinite knowledge
and for a moment I grasped Enlightenment.

Thank You for Gaia.
She somehow sustains seven-billion people without complaining.
I guess that's why she has grown so large.

Thank You for the stars.
A Universe of unknown possibilities,
so that no matter what I imagine, there is always much more.

Thank You for language.
Without it I'd be a naked monkey without a tail...
Hell, that's what I am anyway.

So thank You for curiosity.
The desire to explore and build in this world
is what drives me forward.

Thank You for music, art, dance, and poetry.
They remind me of a place so old
my memory short-circuits and my heart explodes.

Thank You for hands.
Creation is a beautiful force
and I never get enough of it.

Thank You that I get to be Here.
Thank You for another day.
Thank You. Thank You. Thank You.   —*Summer 2012*

38. Lobo
The Year of the Wolf
A eulogy for Sean Armstrong, who awakened the wolf in us all.

The stars have lost their glitter.
There glimmer the remains of drained-out hope in every star
    shimmer that I see.
Moments steal away breaths that flicker between heartbeats in your
    chest, as fleeting existence settles into rest.
You remind me of a dragonfly dancing in the sky with your wings
    tied around me in magic embraces.
Like the nights when light shined through our faces to the *buzzing*
    inside of our soul cases.
Each hug was a gift of the Present's Now, focusing the mind away
    from what or how—distractions—reactions to the Heaven in
    your eyes.
And even now the sky cries.
I've never seen weather fight so hard for the dying as when she knew
    the results, but kept on trying.
Failing, but still buying us more time… More time.

You are an endless song with no refrain.
I never got to explain and the hugs never remained long enough.
I'll never be the same.
Maybe next lifetime. Maybe next time.

I beg my ego to leave so the heart knots can un-weave and release all
    the waterfall waves wrapped into my heart holes.
How can my pulse grow so heavy when my blood has run dry?
How can tears keep filling my fried red eyes?
How can I remember to live Now, or even why I should?

Through the swollen empty ache of our pulses, I confess: I loved you
    the moment your smile rested on my backside, bursting into
    wings on my soul's hide.
Outside, temperatures too cold for June engulf.
I guess too cold for the Summer Moon Wolf, so you're gone.
And yet, I'll see you as soon as the lunar breeze echoes with your
    laughter in the windy trees.

I'll know your heart burst in the first starlight tonight.

I'll feel your breath on the next dragonfly's wings and in every song
the world sings.

But, more than any life lesson I seek to learn from this, my eyes still
burn with empathy road rashes.

My heart still yearns to dust off the ashes of charred lost moments
and reveal one more. Just... one more.

You've started a Greenhouse Butterfly Effect of hurricane change in
our hearts.

You planted seeds before we parted and before this lifetime even
started.

Thank you for finding This Moment.

For you, I'll never leave it again.

Enjoy living in the stars amidst the moonbeams.   —*June 2009*

39. The Greenhouse Effect

I.

Plants grow in a greenhouse; people grow in the Greenhouse Effect.
We gather to plant roots, 'cause we all thrive in abundant Love.
Art awakens sprouts into Life; we come here to be watered.

Our souls rise as the Sun sets until Time stops and even when
the hours overflow from coffee cups, we keep on singing,
because you cannot stop the effect of greens grown in this house.

Each week we find ways to break boundaries and redefine worlds.
Between old jokes and new virgins, this building is bubbling,
full of insurmountable smiles and our shared suffering.

In this greenhouse, we are all the flowers, the shrubs, and the trees,
overgrowing and ready to emerge onto the vast world.
We're a Secret Garden overtaking the Savage Jungle.

Be prepared, my dear world, you have not seen the Beauty of this
Paradise and you are not ready for the perfection of
this Bliss. Come feast with us in evolution and transcendence.

—Winter 2008-09

II.

This Greenhouse breeds butterflies. Broken caterpillars creep in
and fly away later, cloaked in chromatic lotus blossoms.

When Sean Armstrong died, I promised his broken chrysalis that
I would love this flora and fauna the way he taught me to.

This is a grove of ancient forest, a classroom of masters.
Study the rings. We are a library carved into tree trunks.

In this conservatory, we practice metamorphosis.
We shed the layers of our shells as wings grow ever stronger.

Working with such souls is more than I could ever desire.
Thank you, my dearest Greenhouse Effect, for letting me serve you.

—Summer 2012

40. Pleasant at Present

We estimate tomorrow based on yesterday, and define Time by
   mixing the two together.
But Time doesn't exist if you only have Today for comparison.

The line between being human and a human being is thick with
   barbed wire, but many walk along the wrong side for far too long.
Reaching for the placid sunlight of tomorrow's daydreams and
   sacrificing Today with stares that scar their eyes, instead of
   allowing the light to brighten their cerebral cortices.
Enlightenment and insanity are synonyms for parallel paths to the
   same resolutions.
Yet, neither one will bring you closer to the God in yourself—to the
   Heaven of This Holy Moment.

Distractions fill our substandard subconscious.
We can't hear the chirping Earth birds over the scrolling sub-thought
   of absurd words in our heads, because the gravity of our egos is
   sucking us into an early grave.
Fear stream-lines through our ears until we can't hear what's Here.
Our thoughts have been replaced with placebo ideas, preconceived
   by our parents.
The persistent concepts of those that would divide and sell humanity
   to the highest bidder.
But ownership is an idea for the livers of tomorrow and yesterday.

We dope ourselves with pounds of sugarcane that are neurotic
   Novocain on the soul, and forget the true drugs of Life, Breath,
   and Creation behind a crystalline-constructed happiness.
But the ache always returns, so we keep our tongues numb and
   trapped in the dumb hum of television screens.
Yet, I know there is a glistening golden nugget to be mined in the
   crevices of every mind.
When we each find that treasure, we are freed from the rules we hid
   behind.
Resulting in the relief of finally scratching a precariously positioned
   itch.

Life is what happens in your blind spots while you're busy dodging
  potholes in the road.
Escape the myriads of cookie-cutter, mould holds you place yourself
  and others into.
Release *all* expectations.
No one can achieve what you want but you, and you are doing the
  best you can.

Let everything be an unexpected surprise of the present, because
  every chip in today's joys is the result of living in a marbleized
  world constructed with yesterday's yearnings and future fantasies.
Reach for tomorrow, but know that it will never be enough and you'll
  never be better off than you are Right Now.
Heaven is a state of being that you can only reach when you can
  honestly say to yourself:
Today is the best day of my life.   —*Spring 2009*

41. The Clown Car

Somehow, seven-billion humans are surviving on this planet together.
We are too many people, piled in a clown car, wondering why we
    throw elbows in each other's faces and why the driver is having
    trouble steering straight.
Learning to be human is like learning to drive and most of us wreck
    the car eventually.
But rather than broken-down bumper cars, I like to think of us as old
    Chevy Cameros.
Life requires constant maintenance, but Beauty and Trust are things
    you earn with time—like old wine or that radiator you have to
    kick to get working, but it *always* works.
Maybe the world is just waiting for a universal kick start.

These days, no one believes in people anymore.
After funneling faith into the engine of God, Government, and
    Media, we end up abandoned and empty at the side of the road.
It doesn't matter what condition a car is in, they cannot function
    without gas.
That's how so many feel today: out of gas, abandoned, empty, and
    waiting for AAA to come fix it, rather than walk along our
    deserted highways to the gas station that lies *so far away*.

We blame people for the ways they hurt us, but we are all human—
    flawed and struggling the same ways you are.
We throw wrenches at each other trying to "fix" the world, but we
    just end up flinging metal and denting each other's chassis.
The world is held together with string and superglue, because without
    it, the whole engine breaks down and that's what we're afraid of:
Losing our humanity behind the flaws in our understanding.
Handing over the keys to someone who will crash the vehicle.
There is no mechanic to fix the world, so we wake up every morning
    to do things we know we shouldn't have to, treat people in ways
    that hurt them, and go to bed each night wondering if we will
    make the same mistakes tomorrow.

Will we ever understand this human mechanism enough to repair it?

Will we ever trade in these gas guzzlers for the fully renewable Light
of the Sun?

Will we ever forgive the world for the damage it has done to us?

I don't know, but perhaps rather than broken machines, we are stars
covered up with pollution—still shining the same, but no one can
see our light through the smog.

We *feel* depleted, but our tanks are far from empty: We are *gas giants!*

No one makes it out of here dent free, but we don't need to be
"fixed", just cleaned up a bit.

A little wax and polish to bring out that star-shine—little Chevy
Cameros hung on the roads of the sky.

I am no mechanic, just a fool wandering from place to place and
making mistakes at the expense of those around me.

What does it mean to be human?

We just don't have enough time to figure it out before we die.

Maybe that is intentional—forcing us to work together as we
scramble to keep this vehicle working.

We are all just driving through space in a clown car, on a long cosmic
road trip, 93-million miles from the Sun.   —*February 2013*

42. Lady Liberty

I am a *Mona Lisa* painted over the top of dozens of flawed oil layers.
I am hundreds of hidden portraits beneath a small frame.
This Beauty and the Beast society places me in a glass case—an
    immortalized flower that withers every second.
But I am not an enchanted rose, glowing brilliantly every moment
    until the last petal falls.
I am a curse cloaked in magic; I am pain cloaked in a smile.
I am a valley hiding between the mountains of men.
There are no faces of women on Mount Rushmore, so I've often
    chiseled my features to get my image up there.
But I am not marbled abs and sculpted hips; my bust is full of
    chips—puttied and patched to mask my marred surface.
I am the *Venus de Milo*: Goddess of Beauty with arms broken off.
I am the *Winged Victory*: Goddess of War, half shattered, but wings
    still flying in majestic glory.
My heart beats in imperfection, breaking open my skin as it fractures
    the bones of my chest.
But I wear my shortcomings proudly and openly, because my faults
    are the cracks in the Earth where lava flows.
I am not a flaw who must be "fixed".
I have scratched open my canvas on purpose.
I have destroyed the rose that curses me, by breaking the spells of
    this twisted society.
Men are not Michelangelo's *David*, cold and unfeeling.
Women are not manikins that can be moved and modeled to the
    latest trends.
We are flawed, each in our own way.
Ah, but the one mistake in a series of prints makes it priceless.

If you cannot handle my flaws, you do not understand my beauty.
I am Lady Liberty, standing strong with welcoming arms, even as I
    turn green and decay.
My face is memorable the world over.
I stand as a reminder that an artisan is not someone who never makes
    mistakes.
Rather, a true master is someone who knows how to use them.

—Summer 2012

43. Power Paper Wine

My back is broken-down and strapped with twisted tinsel strings that
reflect the flaws they bind, suctioning my wrinkles and pock-
marks in wraps of silvery twine.
But between the strawberry vines that weave from my heart to my
finger lines, there's a clouded concoction bottled and flowing with
red berry wine.

I just want to feel your breath on me—breathing freely.
But these bindings have me ringing and wrought and thinking of
being what I'm not.
And the leprosy has spread to your skin as well, marking your
powdered-precisely, paper covering with rips and tears and tears
for an un-ripened power paper wine.
It tastes of vinegar if you let it sit too long.

I want to be the planter, the picker, the bottler, the drinker, as well as
the drink itself.
Ambitions of fruition that lead to a cracked glass of my own crooked
existence, knocked of center.
Yet, there's the perfect mix in here somewhere, between what I'm
offering and what you need:
Between the sweet poignant taste of your magnificence and my
emptiness.
But I'm torn between whether to cap the cork tight and thus seal the
deal, or enjoy the erupting elating madness that is ensured from
the release of a fully matured masterpiece.

I just want your smile to stretch across orchard miles.
To squish grapes between your toes as I hide in the rows, dancing
and laughing in linguistic Summer seduction.
To sleep in the Sun and ripen so that we may relax into the realness
of ourselves, instead of demands of those dampening desiring
drinkers.
Mixing into the sourest vinegar wine that we can, if that's indeed
what we are meant for.

I just—oh I just want to press my heart to yours!
My red-apple lips reach up to find the boughs of your branches
 wrapped around me in a twisted maze of trunk and treetop.
I want to mix my berry center full to the top in red pop-rocking
 juices, and into a lock with your fizz-bubbling champagne-spring,
 geyser-shooting eruption.
To remove the mounting tension of the underground onto the Earth
 and soak the world with the sweet ripened treat of a delight yet
 un-tasted.
I want to bind my eyes to yours and unwrap the flaws, so that the
 drink drips onto your tongue.
Whether or not it's perfect.

Somehow, we have not even begun to discover the combination of
 ourselves and the creation of that "fruitation".
Let's swap glasses and unwrap the shining tinsel strings to reveal the
 slices in the skin beneath.
I assure you, our strawberry centers will pulse with the purest results
 of explosive distilled dynamite on the taste buds.
With the glittering strings left on the ground behind us, the bottles
 will overflow, and the world will never taste the same.

—*Winter 2008-09*

44. Painting with Memories

It feels like my paintbrush has been stolen from me.
I'm still attempting to make strokes, but nothing is showing up.
So my completely useless canvas stays blank.
I miss you.
I never understood loneliness until you came and left.
It's like being alone in a hall of mirrors, seemingly surrounded by
    people, but none of them can lead me to an exit.
I wish your songs were playing on the intercom, so at least I'd have a
    distraction from my reflections.
Instead I'm left with a head full of massacred words and the *thud* of
    whole poetry bodies dragging down my heart.

Flashes full of memories cover my eyes and I am lost in the energy of
    who I remember you to be.
But the memories are just pictures trying to define Reality and you
    are far beyond that.
If existence were a heartbeat, you would be the pumping.
If substance were a galaxy, you would be a universe.
If everything sings, you would be the silence.
I never understood black holes until I looked into your eyes.
They are proof that something so dark can be so full of light.

In my attempts to fly, I repeatedly stabbed my heart with feathers.
But when thrown into the wind, the makeshift wings only made my
    heart heavier.
And the repetition only ended in damages.
And my heart just ended up full of holes, like big bullet puncture
    wounds on a gun-range target, but this wasn't practice.
Your presence is like sunrays; instead of haphazardly healing my
    holes, you shine into me.
My blemishes become windows to brighten my being.
You're like a lightning zap of love-electricity to bring life back to me.
But now my heart just feels full of holes again.

I think love is like the dinosaurs:
Even with all the facts, we still get it wrong sometimes.
Even with a million predictions, none come close to the truth.

And like those large lizards, it's never fully appreciated until it's gone.
In fact, it may take a catastrophic comet to convince us of its
    importance.

In life, it's not where you go or what you do, it's *who you are with*.
Why else would a god create companions?
Love is only good when given away.
So I guess I can finally say: I miss you.
And I guess I can finally say: I love you.
Because I can only lose *more* at this point.

I suppose I better learn to paint without a brush.
So that while you're away, I can still make masterpieces.

—Winter 2009-10

45. Not in Moderation

Your eyes flicker in dream sleep and I wonder where you are.
The moonlight reflects upon your hair, and I reflect upon it.
We are reflections of the presences around us.
Where am I when no one is looking?
The Moon's beams peer between the blinds—unabashedly examining
    my reflections as I examine hers.
Does her pock-marked skin know how enchanting it is?
We are moons that hold back our light, afraid of our own craters.
But the Moon's glowing scars are brighter than all the stars in the sky.
Why do we fear Beauty?

The Buddha taught moderation in all things, but something keeps me
    from taking his advice: Your eyes—flickering with sleep.
I laugh. Fuck moderation.
I want you *always*. I love you *always*.
If that is the only thing keeping me from Enlightenment, then I'll
    forgo it.
Nirvana is not a land where everything is calculated and planned.
My Heaven requires everlasting and eternal love… *always*.
Not in moderation.

The moonlight catches my eyes as it is covered up by clouds.
I wonder: Are we still shining when clouds cover us up?
How can everything fade away if impermanence is paradoxical?
Do the sparks still shine through our blinds when we close our eyes?
Your breath washes upon me and I press my lips to yours, hoping to
    inhale some of that serenity.
Hoping you will take me to that shore of snores you sailed away to a
    few hours ago.
Finally, my heart slows and my mind-maelstrom subsides.
By the time I drift off to sleep, I am the most Awake I have ever
    been.
Drenched in the Moon's rays and reflecting full brilliance with
    nothing to cover me up.
Where do we go when our eyes close?
Take me there. It's better than any Enlightenment could claim to be.
It is where you are.
                                                    —*Winter 2010-11*

46. Until the Last Grain Falls

Time cycles down the drain like an hourglass.
Ground-up red rocks and blue-moon, shadow sands sift down.
The ground beneath us sinks away like quicksand.
The shifting cinders of earth are unsettling and we perceive the
    change as a loss.
But our growing-pain tears drip into the hole beneath our feet,
    seeding the ground into terraformed green-grass fields.

Soon we will tip the hourglass back over.
In the next era, the sky will be made of sands dripping wastelands
    above us, and the ground will become an endless sky.
The heavens will lie within reach, and the Earth will be untouchable.
(H)our looking glass will be opposite in this world.
The dreams will be the reality and we'll wonder why we keep having
    daymares of working in a little cubicle.
Our hearts will beat outside our chests, so we never have to guess
    each other's emotions.
We'll sweat beautiful crystals of light.
Space will be hot and the suns will be cold.
Our bodies will disintegrate, making our consciousness evaporate
    into water droplets.
The Howl of Wolves will become a color.
The Song of the Whales will be a drug.
The Iridescence of a Dragonfly's Wings will be a feeling.
The next world will be so different that we won't even recognize it
    when it happens.
Our minds will instantly recalibrate to the new climate and convince
    us that it has always been that way.
The shifting of worlds is alchemical: We rearrange the same elements,
    but the reaction is completely different.
Yet, when they are distilled down to their Purest Essence, everything
    is the same.

Times are changing, and I am drifting away with them.
Magicians color Love Pathways on sidewalks so that when we walk
    into the sandstorm chariot, those with a magnifying-glass
    consciousness can analyze it.

Whether you know it or not, this morning was sung in by musicians and will be laid to rest by poets.

Sand paintings of Today were recorded by artists, and soon we'll all dance by moonlight.

In the next phase of the hourglass, suffering will be a concept explained by ballads to help us understand it.

No matter how we stand under this maelstrom of sinking sand, we are all bound to be pulled beneath it.

If you have the imagination to build in the Infinite, wake up in it tonight.

There is a whole world beneath your eyelids where the currency is eye sparkles, and our next project is how to catch lightning in a bottle.

The hourglass sands are circling the drain.

You will need that lightning to spin the sands into a magnifying glass sharp enough to analyze your mind.

Leave the world you are in and create a new one.

We are waiting for you.

And we will keep waiting, until the Last Grain Falls.   —*Spring 2011*

47. The Bear

Your soul reminds me of dew on lavender leaves, dripping with
    melodies in the tones of violin strings.
The beating of your heart brings unicorns *trumpeting* from the forest
    in full force.
The silk of your skin was spun by a million glowing caterpillars,
    creating a cocoon meant for the butterfly that lies dormant in you
    somewhere.
You have the sense of adventure of one who has never known an
    anchor and rides wherever the wind goes.
You jump into the worst situations—with a spunky appetite for new
    and unknown—because they give the best results.
Confidence forces its way from your hands and feet as your actions
    spread like oil onto those around you.

But my gentle grizzly, you have fallen asleep in the cave of a lie.
Surrounding yourself with that which is comfortable in exchange for
    your explosive self.
You've allowed yourself to be lulled to sleep because Winter
    promises to be cold and you'd rather sleep through the struggle in
    the known and expected than wrap your mind around Reality.
I wish you'd awaken with the roar I know you have inside, crumbling
    the caverns you've crept into, awakening into twice who you were
    before the sleep, feeding off the rest you've received, and rocking
    the whole world off its axis and onto yours.
How do I show you that though it's harder, the struggle is worth
    every moment?
Because you own it. Because you live it.

My friend, you can sleep in your cave, locked in your dreams, waiting
    for a better day to emerge that may never come.
While butterflies erupt in gardens outside, you can dream of the
    incredible imaginary world of the extraordinary.
Meanwhile, I can only ask you, in the whisper of a stored acorn
    waiting for water:
Come back. Come back.   —*Winter 2008-09*

48. Her Name Was Curiosity

I saw a butterfly today and it broke my heart.
She drank dandelion daydreams and transcended the ordinary.
I couldn't help but wonder if she was the last of her species.
Why do we hate and destroy?
Hate is rape of the heart and we're all getting our sick fixes off of
    degradation and handcuffs.

I long for the first days of Creation.
The Garden of Eden makes sense to me.
Though I know I couldn't just Be.
Forbidden Fruit is the type of thing I get off on.
Call me Eve, but curiosity is one of the most admirable traits I've
    seen.
I love when it gleams through eyes of those glowing with Life.

It is the questions that keep us living.
We thirst for the nectar in the Flowers of Life, pollinating all day for
    a few flourishing fruits.

I saw a butterfly today and it broke my heart.
Her name was Curiosity.
Perhaps she will return when we have transcended these ordinary
    words.   —*Fall 2009*

49. Troublesome Tongues
Tribute to Phone Sex

Baby, I'm calling you tonight to keep my tongue talking.
Lately, I have grown restless stalks that have replaced the crops of
your kisses.
My tongue misses traveling along teeth-paved roads to new places.
The new spaces found when tracing along lip lines.
The confines we escape when our tongues run along each other and
we discover dreams hidden beneath the covers.
My tongue hungers for the mountain ridges and valleys of your ear
folds, holds me in contempt as I attempt to think and sink into
the never-ending.
It wants to touch your skin and find a way into your soul.
Wants to graze along collar bones and soak in your tones.
Use your torso as a saltlick and stick to your flesh like it's in need of
the nutrition.
Treat you like a plantation and I'm there dying from starvation.
I want to pull down whole fruit trees and feed by sucking on the
succulent seeds of your body.
I want to treat your kisses like fishes and begin eating meat again just
to sample your midsection.

I'm feeling kinda frisky and my curiosity is getting the best of me.
I'm like a cat that can't quit the string when my tongue clings to you
so tightly you can't get away.
And let me tell you, we're going to earn that catnap, though when
this cat's got your tongue, playtime is never really done.
Honey, my tongue is a busy bumblebee with a sting that burns
ecstasy.
It makes beats so hot they melt nuclear winters.
Sings steamy strands of treble-clef trouble, while doubling heartbeats
and pumping hard bass lines.
It wants to sing you praise and amaze you with the notes it reaches,
tip flicking forward to rhythms that imprison your vision into
ethereal worlds of wisdom.
I long for the demise of your eyes as they lock closed when the
tension rises.

My tongue wants to wrap around your fingers and linger on your
    stomach.
Make magic among your wrinkles and soak into your contours.
Pour into your pores and adore your back side.
Slide along hip lines and define your borders.
Lick over your flesh and cover your chest.
Feel your breath on the wetness.
Pump sweat from your skin as you begin to moan.

My love, I can't leave you alone!
My tongue is aching to do battle on your ribcage by fighting with
    freckles and slicing through soft spots.
I recommend you come willingly, though resisting may make things
    more interesting.
So, my dear, we've got talking to do.
Help me untie my troublesome tongue and find some sanity.
Really, all I'm asking you, baby, is will you please…
Stay awake with me?   —*Spring 2010*

50. Ghost-Self

There's a secret part of me I've kept tucked under the covers of my
  chest for years.
A long time ago, she saw monsters crawling around her and fear
  drove her deep inside.
She lies there in darkness, masked by closed doorways and blankets
  that make her feel safe.
She's too scared to approach the beasts outside.
Someone told her that these savages would consume her and she
  believed that isolation was the only safe way.

After I hid her away, I pretended to be perfect, letting this little child
  rest inside, while my face played the part of a chameleon.
My color reflected my surroundings so everyone would like me:
Sweet as orange peaches today.
Yellow sunshine happiness tomorrow.
The brown of solid tree trunks when around my family.
Cool blue when I wanted to seduce someone.
I could be anything, and I loved the acceptance I attained by it.
I wasn't faking: These were just different parts of me.
It was a good story. I believed it strongly.
Tucked myself into it regularly, comforted and safely wrapped inside
  while even I believed my lies.
But in reality, I was afraid to be anything that wasn't accepted fully...
  even when I was alone.
What if I wasn't good enough?
Well that was a secret I kept from myself—stashed on the shelf
  behind dusty book jackets.
I would never open the pages that described my insecurity, and I was
  content with sheets pulled over my head, cutting holes for eyes,
  disguised in my ghost-costume.
But I focused so hard on being something specific that I forgot that
  there's actually a person in there to express.
Even if my outer image is exactly who I want her to be, there is still a
  lonely child inside, afraid to go play.

We create judgments so that we know exactly what is expected of us.
Surprises are frightening.

But we confine ourselves with decisions we make about other people,
    and judgment is a two-way window that we both agree upon.
We shape each other into neat little stereotype boxes and cliché
    packages to place distance between us—creating fake people with
    fake interactions, and now, there are six people in the room
    instead of just two:
There's me and you.
But there's also who I project and your interpretation of her.
Plus your reflection, and my decisions about you.

I've chosen a ghost costume and you've chosen another monster.
No wonder we can't understand each other.
People are happy to lie to you, if you ask them to.
But as long as we keep analyzing each other, comparing ourselves to
    giants, we misinterpret infants for villains.
Our world mimics *Where the Wild Things Are*, and we all act like
    monsters to avoid being eaten.
Pulling disguises over our heads and lurking in darkness.
Creating a fortress to protect us from each other.

The world is a playground.
The only boxes that exist are full of sand waiting for us to dig tunnels
    to China, where they walk upside down.
I'd like to tell you that everything is different now—that I pulled
    open the shutters and went out to play in the yard—but the truth
    is: I'm still scared.
However, I finally found the doorway and I brushed the dust off the
    stories that contain the real me.

I'm sick of sleeping, screaming, and repressing myself.
You may be a monster, but that will make you better at digging holes.
I'll take the risk for the chance to be me and the chance to see you.
From there, it's just practice.
I'll conquer my fear eventually.
The Great Wall awaits me.
I hope to see you on the flip side.   *—Spring 2011*

51. Scaredy Cats

Jungle-cat creatures hide in tree cover:
A canopy of ego on the outside to protect them from the fictitious
    lightning storms above.
While itchy-tick-fear vermin crawl through their fur walls, corrupting
    the mind with brain-infesting hate calls.
Meanwhile, the tall trees are rotting with trickery and termites.
They only reach to such great heights because of the fallen friends
    that rest at their feet.
They fight whole forests thinking it's better to be bigger, but the
    most triumphant tree trunk is not always the tallest, the last one
    standing, or even always right.
Kitties(kiddies) afraid of dark places will never travel into deep inner
    spaces.
Self-deception ego trees keep us free from the real person we hate:
    ourselves.
Delusion seems a savior to lives stained with pain, so many resort to
    escapism thoughts, constructs like acid rain.
But those corrosive concepts of money and fame are just temporary
    anti-truth goggles to a world gone insane.

We're lost in thoughts of ourselves and believe their existence proves
    self-confidence.
We long for the ego trees to fall and reveal Real Sunlight
    Enlightenment.
Yet, we jungle-cat creatures hide in our tree covers, propping up
    planks to shove away Love.
Inflated sense of self seems the only way to shield the snakes that
    slither through the trees.
But few vines are serpents, and fear only forces us to delay from
    climbing through to a Brighter Day where the Sun blazes at every
    moment.

We jungle-cat creatures hide in tree cover, longing for escape.
We know we could rise above by tearing down branches.
Stick by stick pick down the wicked strength deception.
But broken branches lead to breakdowns and not many can take
    down a whole forest.

Luckily, the medicine is stronger than the sickness.
Love is like a disease for the trees: It purges a forest and kills all the
fleas by forcing them down, under their own weight.

Jungle-cat creature, you are perfect and powerful, with eyes that
reflect a soul like Excalibur: unconquerable and beautiful!
Once all barriers are broken, you can run free into the Field of
Dreams.
Limitless—as you were meant to be.   *—Fall 2009*

52. Answer

Why am I here? To Love.
And every day is a success.
Before I was born, I fell in love with Love and I can't give up until
    everyone has felt it.
My true heart's desire is to fall for every person I meet.
Je suis en amour avec tout le monde!
Life allows me plenty of opportunities to do so.
Sometimes we forget how beautiful the world is.
We get stuck in boredom, apathy, or fear, not realizing what illusions
    they all are.
But our perceptions are mere wrinkles on the Great Blanket of Life.
We fixate on the folds and hate the imperfections, but the cloth itself
    is perfect, and a simple shake of the fabric can change everything.

Yet, rather than change things, we run away from Reality.
Mother Culture is pimping out dreams, because to dream you have to
    be sleeping.
This system is like a prostitute who says she's in love, when she's
    really just screwing us for our money.
Governments assign social-security numbers so they can look at us as
    numbers.
We are not humans on that virtual screen and it's easy to control
    something when you can just push the delete key.
We think that just because we participate in our brainwashing that
    somehow we are not still being brainwashed.

We love to give away our power.
We elect others above ourselves and blame them for our problems.
It's easier to attack someone else for not doing what we ask, than to
    do it ourselves.
Easier to blame Divinity for not creating the world we want, than to
    do it ourselves.
This world is a mess because we choose to make it that way.
Blame whomever you want, but that is the fact.

We use the great skill called "free will" to force our desires on the
    world and then complain when things don't go our way.

But independence is what a cancer cell has against its own body:
It divides endlessly for itself, at the expense of all around it.
A single confused cell can kill a trillion others and itself.

It is quite egocentric to be unhappy in This Moment.
This Great Work is not some cheap novel needing corrections.
It's a masterpiece thought out meticulously with purity in every word.
After all, God is a Word and Language is Creation.
So please, be careful what you say.
I don't appreciate a world where: "She's a bitch" or "He's a douche
     bag."
Why do we think we are helping people when we hurt them?
There is no glory in demeaning others and I don't see how you can
     complain about their actions until yours are perfect.

We dream of being invincible, but we are not gods. We are God.
We dream of wings, but believe we are only caterpillars.
We sleep in cocoons, awaiting the day we can Awaken.
We want to be Butterflies, not realizing we already are.
Wake up!
Life is just waiting for you to discover that you can already fly.
And when you do, She will clap like a child that has watched Her
     little furry caterpillar discover it is actually an Eagle.

An angel once told me, "Art is the Answer."
Instead of breaking others down, build something up.
Flood this world with creation:
Make every movement a dance, every sentence a poem, and every
     breath a song.
To create a better world, we must first *create*.
This great galaxy of ours is a mere chakra of God that spirals in
     rhythm with the whole Universe.
Open up to the magnificence of your own creations and make
     something worth having.

Why are you here?
The Answer is far simpler than the fabrications we've been
     brainwashed and conditioned to look for: To Love. To Help. To
     Serve. To Be. To Exist. To Experience. To Create. To Connect.

There is nothing getting in your way!
The new world is here. Right Now.
Greet every morning in Perfection.
Shake out the wrinkled cloth of perception.
Fall in Love.
Enjoy this elaborate novel.
Stretch your wings, dear Eagle.
We are already There.
Accept your power and realize that you are personally responsible for
   your world.
Create and live like a fluid work of art, because you are.

Welcome to Heaven.   *—Fall 2011*

53. Math = Sex

I've been flipping through pages of math equations and through my
   precise calculations I've discovered something overwhelming:
Math is sex.
You don't believe me?
Well listen up, because I'm going to teach you a few things worth
   learning:

Instead of getting lost among lines and numbers, let's add figures
   together.
Let's lower the root of our numerical base until one plus one still
   equals one, because those are some figures I'd like to line up
   together.
Let's go in rhythms of steady algorithms until we can derive all
   possible solutions.
There's only one answer to the questions I'm asking and they all
   involve you and me stripping away the unnecessary and solving a
   few variables.
There is the perfect ratio of me to you and I want to trace parallel
   lines on your sides to figure out how they intersect with mine.
I want to try all your angles, capture divergent lines, and measure
   your tongue with mine.
Am I being too graphic?
I can graph us together if you like, flip it on its side and add the z-
   axis.
Let's match our dimensions until our separations grow together and
   we're left asking about y?
It may be irrational, but I find myself tracing fractals in your irises
   until I get lost in the Infinity that lies there.
I'm inspired by the sacred geometry of your smile:
A sacred set of symbols that seduces me regularly.
The golden mean is spiraling into our centers and soon we'll be left
   with perfection as our infinite proportion.
We move too fast for reality, but my projections can foresee the
   ending when we pass the final threshold of our current confines.
Do you get what I'm saying?
Let's redefine the "slide rule."
Let's figure in the x-factor.

Let's discover imaginary numbers.
Let's quantify obscure amounts until black holes connect together
    and we wander into worm holes of the impossible.
I don't mean to tangent, but my sines and your cosines are directing
    us in different directions and I just want to figure out how a + b
    can always equal a way to c into your heart.
And even if you only understand a fraction of what I'm saying, I
    hope it's enough to balance our equations.

No matter how we combine the statistics, you and I yield some tricky
    mathematics.
So come play mathematician with me.
We'll start with our addition, we'll end with our subtraction, and
    somewhere in the middle, we'll devise a way to multiply
    heartbeats.
We might get confused and there might not be any answers when
    we're done, but we'll pretend to know what we're talking about
    and speak endless innuendos when we don't.
So come with me.
I'll show you some sexy statistics, you'll bring the pi, and after it's all
    squared away, we'll circle each other's minds until we understand
    the endlessness of it.
If we ever need the precise calculations, we'll form radial lines to the
    curves of our bodies and determine the areas of our skin's
    circumference.
At the very minimum, I promise we'll laugh at all the similarities
    between math and sex.   —*Spring 2011*

54. Puzzle

I don't understand the cryptic stares from your treasure-chest eyes.
You're locked in behind the sockets.
Pleading for me to wrench open the sunken pockets.
Yet, you flash warning signs that threaten possibility with a pistol.
I don't understand the confliction, so I assume it's only a warning
    and taunt your itchy trigger finger to fire.
I should leave it alone, but those deep glistening onyx eyes are
    soaking up all the light in the room and casting shadows on
    everyone who walks through the door.
But you can't see through those light soaked eyes because somehow
    you've wrapped a rubber band around the cover of your heart and
    hid the whole thing between stained sheets, a broken spring
    mattress, and a life of excess.
I want to rip off that damned band and shoot it into your stubborn
    heart!
To reveal understanding onto the umbra that eclipses your soul with
    unimportant traumas.

But all this calculation is just speculation on my half of the equation.
Maybe one plus one actually equals zero affection from your heart.
Maybe the enigma I perceive is an emulation of emotions on the
    outside so that you may get to my inside.
A vacuum that is sucking up my star-struck soul into a black hole of
    exponential gravity so that I'll never find it again.
Maybe you're no longer in possession of the map to your heart and I
    must now travel the labyrinth alone in search of my own solution.
At this point I've considered every code, key, cheat, map, answer, and
    trick to translate your hieroglyphics with the hope that one will
    crack the riddle.
I'm beginning to suspect that figuring out your cryptic eyes may be
    the death of me, the coffin, the nail; gravedigger too.
A labyrinth-like tomb where I'll be trapped with an eternity to figure
    out how to get free.
I'm beginning to wonder if there's a workable solution to this
    seemingly simple Rubik's Cube, or if the stickers have been
    randomly mixed up and replaced.

Perhaps I'm over-thinking all of this esoteric analysis.

Maybe as you look at me you are just wishing for the codex to my encryption.

Could it be that there is no final solution to any puzzle?

We're all just trying to ram the pieces together wherever they fit in the hope of completion.

Learning that true happiness comes in the solving and the less the puzzle looks like the original picture, the more interesting it is.

—Winter 2008-09

55. Radiation

For Jonathan Hague

The Sun cracks wide-open as a soul leaves the planet Earth.
The Solar Star expands His core to make more room.

Over the next four months, the Sun will shed flares from His cape.
He will radiate the Earth until we all understand the strength of this
    one we lost.

My friend, you radiated so much light.
It only makes sense that your light was taken by radiation.

Now you live in the Sun, radiating back to us for eternity.

—August 2013

56. The Feeling

There is a Universal lifeline that drips like an IV directly into my
heart:
An invisible solution that delivers Love intravenously, like Venus
dripping deliberately into my being.
There is a beauty in life that goes unseen.
It is a feeling.
Something that words can never know, but the heart can never
forget.
This feeling is our umbilical cord(chord) to the Universe.
It is bottles of the galaxy's best moments chugged repeatedly and
deliberately.
It is endless film reels of the Real casting heavenly scenes on the
heart, but it is the knowledge that a photograph can never capture
this feeling.
The physical world has never known this internal place, this internal
space that is more expansive than the edges of Time itself.
You know what I'm describing. We all do.
But to understand it with the mind is to bastardize the essence of it.
This is a soul-stopping beauty beyond comprehension that breaks our
chains the second it seizes us.
It is the substance we are all searching for in the skies and the
medicine that heals every sickness.
It is the moment that you love someone who does absolutely nothing
for you, and thus know pure, unadulterated innocence.
It is the second when simplicity arrests everything around you and
you cannot walk away.
It is a bumble-bee sleeping on a sunflower.
It is the way the wind blows leaves in circles as you walk.
It is every word that has gone unspoken.

This feeling is the microscope that reveals what we are truly made of.
It peels away the outer-shield and shows the molecules of the soul.
This feeling makes us fall deeply in love with Life.
It is the slingshot pulled back waiting for the chance to fire.
It is the desire to connect and accept everyone we meet, because
when we love, we discover inner angels, but when we judge, we
strap people's wings back, and hate the fact that they can fly.

This feeling is the idea that we live among angels and gods; we just
    miscast them as demons.
That we each radiate sunlight, but clouds cover us up.
This feeling is knowing the value of happiness and the fact that there
    is no telescope imaginable that can analyze a smile.
It is an inner candle that you can pass on without ever diminishing
    your own light.
You have a right to this feeling.
We are each born with this feeling, but daily brainwashing steals it
    from us.
Most of us have lost it completely.
We walk as empty zombies hungering for something, but we don't
    quite know what we are looking for, so we yearn for more of that
    little something we already possess.

So here is my gift to you.
Though, you own it already and all of this is just a reminder:
A memory that is so old you almost forgot.
A place that shows up in your dreams every night, but you can't quite
    recall it in the morning.
Here is that feeling——

Now… *gulp, guzzle, imbibe, indulge.*
Sip, slosh, slurp, and *swig* it down.
Get drunk.
Inebriate yourself so deeply that you never come back.
Then, infect a friend with it.
Share it everywhere.
Drug everyone.
Succumb to that seducing vibe that lives inside and never forget it.
Don't be shy.
This is the reason why you were born.
You are the stars when the Sun is out.
Don't be afraid of darkness, it only makes you brighter.
Experience your brilliance and shine on.
Remember who you are.
An entire galaxy is made of people like you.   *—Fall 2011*

57. Thoughts!
A Fish Story

I sit on the banks of a great ocean.
My fishing pole dangles far out in the waters
and I sleep peacefully by the wayside.

Day-dreaming as I watch the lure
bob gently up and down.
I enjoy true serenity.

Suddenly, the pole reels and I snap to attention.
I grab the rod and start to spin the crank around and reel it in.
Wrenching and reeling, I fight this Super Fish.

It pulls; I pull.
It gives a little; I pull harder. I give a little; it pulls back.
Pulling and pulling—an epic battle.

Ah, but I know the fish will tire before I do; I relax.
I bring it closer and closer until I can pull it out of the water.
Success! I remove the hook and let the fish free.

Relaxing back into my meditation.
Peaceful until another fishy thought
gets caught by the hook of my awareness.

Relax.
Catch the fish
and let it go.   *—Summer 2012*

58. More Waterlogged Words

There is a lake in our chests called Truth.
It is a bottomless Cave of Wonder found by gazing between closed
    eyes and open hearts.
I have been there a few times, but never jumped in.
Sometimes I cast my reel into this pond from afar, but the magic
    lamps I seek lie too deep.
I have yet to gain the courage to indulge in its Beauty.
I dare not dip my toes in for fear that I will never leave again.
One time I captured a sparkle in my eye from the Sun reflecting on
    the surface, but I lost it when I attempted to put it in a cage.

What is Truth?
We write guesses on pages and carelessly cast them into the waters,
    ripping papers out of ourselves as bait for the treasures within.
There are books littering the serene Lake of Truth, thrown by those
    who hesitate at the shoreline—paper leaves floating with soggy
    words that no one can read anymore.
The longer they sit there, the more useless they become.
It is in this I finally understand that the silence of ripples says more
    than my waterlogged words ever can.

Some have no problem visiting paradise and returning back, but most
    get trapped in the caverns, worshipping the riches they contain.
I want to go deep and explore the gem-encrusted caves that sparkle
    below the surface until I find a way to bring a piece back.
It is more likely that I will dive so deeply that I run out of air.
We are unable to glimpse the enormous piles of gold without greed.
Taking a single Jewel of Truth seems inadequate once we view
    endless mountains of them.
So I stand on the banks of Truth, writing riddles about the
    possibilities beneath.
Some stomp freely in the tide, catching treasures in jars.
They return to us with proof of the miracles, but many only see
    muddy sludge.
But a few of us come to understand that the waters themselves are
    the prize, the jewels are the distraction, and just bathing in the
    pool is the point of it all.   —*July 2013*

59. The Tortoise and the Hare

When I was a child, I thought wings were hidden beneath my
    shoulder blades and I always stood up straight in case they ever
    wanted to come out.
They never did.
It was then I learned not to try too hard for the things I want,
    because it is easier to attain the things I don't.
And irrational dreams won't get you anything.
It seems being human is the only thing that gets worse with practice.

Baby rattlesnakes don't know how to control their poison.
They release it all every time they fight.
Living each moment like their last.
Elder serpents learn to ration their passion:
Measure each move you take, so you can always make another one.

Fables always foretell this same story:
"Slow and steady wins the race."
Don't try too hard to achieve first place or you'll end up in last.
Bursts of energy require that you stop to nap, and that's when the
    world will pass you.

Like the ant who stored arduously getting ready for Winter, leaving
    the lazy grasshopper to die without shelter.
I hear over and over I must work and prepare.
There's no time for this hare to sleep.
There's no time for this grasshopper to play.
Incessant negations say:
"There is no easy way. Keep your wings tucked beneath your
    shoulders, back bent forward. Walk toward the end with eyes cast
    down. Don't waste energy on anything but that final line, because
    that is the only way you will ever reach it. Slow and steady wins
    the race. You must work your life away if you hope to place."
But our pacing will not stop our aging.
Working steadily for a finish line will not buy us more time.

Grasshoppers only live for one season; they die after Summer.
So why prepare for a winter that will never come?

Hares get to sleep, while turtles are slaves to the home on their back.
Grasshoppers jump and chirp and sing, while ants follow their leader
    blindly.
Which one is really living?

No matter how slow and steady our speed, we're still racing.
Focusing everything on winning.
We will all get to the end, sure, but at what cost?
The wings will never burst from our back-blades if we are determined
    to walk.
We can dedicate our lives to this competition.
But by the time we've won, we've already passed the finish line.

—April 2010

60. No Wonder Kids Are So Smart

I could live lifetimes in the things I've learned from nursery rhymes. They taught me that:

If you climb up the water spout, you may be washed out, but you should always crawl up again.

The black sheep must give three bags full of their wool away, but at least there is a demand for it, and that's more than I can say for the white sheep.

When the crazy cat won't stop playing that fiddle and the cows are flying over the Moon, it's best to be the dish running away with the spoon.

If I follow Jack, I'll end up like Jill, who also fell down the hill.

While we're working on the railroad all the livelong day, someone's in the kitchen with Dinah, enjoying that old banjo. And that really doesn't seem fair, but at least all of us are singing, even if it's not together.

The farmer of the dell takes a wife, who takes a child, who takes a nurse, who takes a cow, who takes a dog, who takes a cat, who takes a rat, who takes the cheese. But in the end, the cheese stands alone. (We're all owned by someone. Unless you're the big cheese, but then you are alone. And between you and me, I'd rather be owned than alone.)

The cradle will rock, the treetops may break, and we'll all die. But that shouldn't keep you awake at night; in fact, it's an idea you can rock yourself to sleep to.

And finally, these tell-all tales explained that whether we're marching two by two, or three by three, or even four by four, the reason we're marching into the ground is that we're all just trying to get out of the rain.   —*April 2010*

61. A Letter to the Leaders

My dear leaders of the world,
You have wrapped us up in thick ropes, tied in sailor's knots.
You have locked us within safes and hidden the combination behind
  Cerberus's vicious mouths.
You have blindfolded our eyes and silenced our pleas behind screams
  of tortured prisoners.
You have restricted our souls behind controls.

My dearest ones,
We asked you to guide our wandering hearts to pasture.
Like sheep so trusting of our shepherds, we followed you along crags,
  canyons, and steep cliffs—traipsing along in blissful ignorance.
I cannot blame you for guiding us to the Gates of Hades.
For placing our hands into the chains of the ferry—smiling as you
  covered our eyes with golden coins meant to pay for our passage.
I cannot blame you for guiding us deep into the Underworld as we
  blindly trusted your empty oaths and promises of gold.
I am not blaming you in all of this.
It was a poor choice to follow so blindly.
I can only ask you:
What will you do with your leadership?
Where will you guide us with such strength?
Who will you be when power tempts your hands to sail us all into the
  River Styx?
How many hearts have you dashed upon rocks to bribe the boatman?
I am not claiming any folly on your part, but if you cannot yet face
  Death with confidence and grace, how will you ever face Life?

We do not ask you to be Prometheus, sacrificing your souls to bring
  fire to humanity.
We do not ask you to be Sisyphus, rolling a boulder up a hill forever
  to pay for your crimes.
We do not ask you to turn over the reigns of Death's chariot and
  follow the Frightening Night Mares of Charon into the depths of
  Hell itself to atone for your sins.
But my dearest ones, you own the world.
In that, you are Zeus's thunderbolt meant to spark fire in the

sagebrush of our hearts.
When we could all be resting among Olympians feasting on
 ambrosia, you instead lead us to the glowing ghost pools of Pluto.
You remind me of the beautiful Achilles, dipped in the River Styx—
 invulnerable except for your ankle and therefore destined to be
 destroyed by it.
We made you our leaders, given ultimate power and strength; we did
 not realize this made it your Fate to be destroyed by it.

I am sorry for putting you in this blight, but you possess great power.
Now show me what you will do with it.
If you cannot carry the burden of Atlas, holding the world on your
 shoulders, please step down.
I know very few who could hold such weight without collapsing.
And I have only the fondest respect for you in trying.

—February 2013

62. Ravings of a Madman

If I have ever said anything true, it was not because I thought of it.
My mind is a tropical oasis with many buried treasures.
But if I have unburied Truth there, it was because I followed a map.

I am a baby of Gaia's earth and the Sun's fire, filled with a body of
  water and the wind that animates my breast.
Altogether, I am a clay pot in the hands of a Master.
I will be set and ready just in time for the final kiln of cremation.
For now, I am the putty that fills in the broken walls of God's
  Tavern.
If I have ever held Truth, I was probably so drunk that I spilled half
  of it.

I am leaving scraps of myself on the ground like a careless litterbug.
I sew a patchwork blanket onto my skin and attempt to warm those
  suffering in the cold.
I am a seamstress stitching myself together with leftover fragments
  the world hands to me.
If I have found Truth, it was given to me in garbage bags that others
  threw to the curb.

I am homeless and wandering the streets of the gods.
I am also the CEO of my own soul.
I am the rags-to-riches-to-rags-to-riches-to-rags cycle of a top.
I am the spinning toy of Divinity that maintains balance through
  continuous movement.
If I have struck upon Truth, I ran into it in my attempt to exist.

I wish God's notebook was left next to me on the bus, though I
  might not understand it.
Maybe They left within us, painting calligraphy answers on our
  brains.
When we open our minds wide enough, we can read it.
If I have ever spoken Truth, it fell out of my mouth in handwritten
  fragments of the Universe that immediately blew away in the
  wind.

I am a Seeker of Truth, but I would happily follow others if our
leaders were wise and compassionate.
A wise sheep understands that it is better to follow an even wiser
shepherd.
But only a fool follows a fool.
If gurus did not have followers, they would be long-forgotten
homeless men.
I hope that I am wise-enough to follow such people.
But if I have ever known Truth, I probably let it walk away as a lost
opportunity.

Thus far I have forged my own path through the weeds, stumbling
and completely lost.
The notorious "Road less traveled" has been a real pain in the ass.
But Truth is obsolete when spoken and if you follow someone else
the entire way on the beaten path, you will end up beaten on the
path, drunk on heatstroke, and spinning faster than the top of the
world.
If I have uncovered Truth, it was lying in the sand as I walked
between oases.

I am a vagabond.
I don't know anything.
I stumble across the answers right as the questions arise.
I do not know the method that will pull me through the shaman's eye
of a needle, but I know I will receive the gold coin of Truth right
as the toll is due.
But if I have ever known anything true, I probably spent it on my
next meal.

These are the ramblings of a madman, scrawled on paper and
rehearsed to accent their perceived importance.
If any of these words are true, they should be shredded and thrown
away, before anyone attempts to follow them.   —*April 2013*

63. This Is a Poem About Life

I accidentally strangled my pet parakeet, when I was five, while trying
    to help it; I killed a cockatiel with forgetfulness; and chemical-
    induced sleep sterilized my dog's eyes.
And yet, though its genes run in every being, I still don't know what
    death means.

My extended family was dead by the age of twelve.
I still don't know what death means.

My best friend is 105-years-old. He is deteriorating more every day,
    body returning to the grave before he has left it.
I still don't know what death means.

Sean Armstrong died in 2009, taking my hope for humanity with him.
    I tattooed a yin-yang on my ankle so he could live forever.
I still don't know what death means.

Animals go extinct at the rate of dinosaurs. Rainforests are
    deflowered daily. One-billion people starve.
I still don't know what death means.

Movies and videogames kill billions of fake people; wars kill
    thousands of real people.
I still don't know what death means.

There is an America–sized continent of plastic garbage off the coast
    of Hawaii. The Blue Tuna are kept off the endangered species list
    because we cannot survive without them.
I still don't know what death means.

The world's oldest person was recorded at 122-years-old; the
    Methuselah Tree is 4,843-years-old; the Earth is 4.5-billion-years-
    old; the Universe is 13.75-billion-years-old; the U.S. deficit is 15.7-
    trillion-dollars; I am 25.
I don't know what death means.

I have seen so many live as if they will live forever, but we all die, and
    because of that, life is sacred; I will not hurt you assuming an
    afterlife will resolve our differences. There is a blatant, unresolved
    fact staring us all in the face:
None of us knows what death means.

Yet, we listen to the stories of strangers who tell us to give away our
    lives on the dollar. We give away our lives for a dollar.
Though we don't know what death means.

I have seen lives wasted in lethargy though the Sun drips lucidity
    onto our tongues and we taste it every morning like a gumdrop.
    Sometimes Today has the flavor of Desperation, sometimes it has
    the flavor of Retribution, but it always *always* tastes of Beauty,
    because Right Now is perfection. But Apathy overpowers many
    because they wait until tomorrow to sample Today when it is
    rotten, vapid, and plain.
They do not know what death means.

When I died at the age of 20, I was so scared God sent me back. I
    saw the True Beauty of Divinity and it terrified me. I now picture
    death fully every morning, so next time I won't be afraid. The
    other side of the veil is the most beautiful brilliance I have ever
    witnessed, and I long to return there.
I still don't know what death means.

I have had many chances since to go on to my death, but I sacrifice
    that honor to be here with you. I sacrifice Eternity to whisper the
    wind's secrets into your hearts.
Because I still don't know what death means.

So I will go to my end knowing I loved as many people as I could, as
    much as I could, for as long as I could. That I served those I met
    with everything I had and that my love took a piece of me. That I
    assisted every human in the construction of their erector set,
    rather than tear them down.
Because I still don't know what death means.

I will not drift into old age as a broken roller coaster. I will slide into
   death full force, like a baseball player propelled into home,
   covered in dirt and debris. I will meet my end knowing there was
   nothing else I could do here, because for all I know, we treat
   people terribly and then everything ends.
   For all I know, we treat people terribly and then everything ends.
   I will not treat people terribly in case everything ends.
Because I still don't know what death means.

In my heart there is a black quartz crystal called the World Soul; it
   sings in the key of Be. In my veins runs God's golden blood; it
   reminds me to "Be Positive." Yet, my atoms vibrate with the
   same components as a corpse.
I still don't know what death means.

A life well lived is the only way death means something. So I will
   treat you with love and respect every day. Because leaving this
   world better than I found it, on a day that is better than the one I
   was born on is the only way death means something.
With that, perhaps I finally know what death means.

—Summer 2012

64. Valley of the Shadow of Wind

*"Even though I walk through the Valley of the Shadow of Death,
I will fear no evil, for You are with me."* —*Psalm 23:4*

We sip stale coffee as the winds of Time billow outside.
The conversation melts minutes like Salvador Dali illusions.
But this exquisite moment is cracked open with a phrase.
You whisper, "I do not believe in God."

I believe you, but tell me, do *you* believe in the wind?
That blustering breeze outside is not just a passing flurry.
It is an invisible dust containing every planet in the Universe.
Can you believe in a big-bang powder birthed from oneness?

Do you believe in the gust that pushes us from our mothers' wombs?
The first gasps we scream into existence?
Or the bewitching whisper of language?
Do you believe in a typhoon called creation?

Do you believe in the gentle zephyr of a lover?
The soft cherry-blossom snores of an infant?
Or the memory of sweet perfume on the air?
Do you believe in the whirlwind called Love?

Do you believe in an invisible force called "Gravity"?
Or a dodge ball's momentum and the *woosh* of "nothing-but-nets"?
Can you fathom Time's invisible hands blowing along?
Or the concept of intangible power?

Do you believe in the fluid motions of your body?
A suit of a trillion cells that move as you move.
So exact that you fail to see their marionette strings:
A dancer dancing you.

Can you believe in the harp strings of your being?
We are Great Looms of quark fibers and DNA strands, threading the
   soul to the body.
There is music whispered by the shutter of blinking of eyelashes.

Can you believe in the sultry song of Life?

Do you believe in your mother?
Your breaths unified as she rocked you in the boughs of her belly.
Fifteen to twenty-percent of pregnancies end in miscarriage.
Can you believe there was a reason you were not one of them?

Each time you breathe you draw the Universe's specs into your lungs.
These fragments form mini-universes in your bloodstream.
Existence is a yo-yo, sleeping until it returns to the Great Palm.
We all long to return to the cradle of our origin.

When I subtract Spirit from existence, there is no wind to animate
     our breath.
Consciousness is a passing night gale that falls away.
The tornado of creation always ends with destruction.
This poem is an accident, flickering like a candle's flame.

If you mean that God is not some dude in the sky, I agree.
I would not live in a box that small if I were all-powerful.
Science asks for one free miracle: "Everything comes from nothing."
Well that idea requires a faith that I do not possess.

But I have seen the wind in your soul when you exhale.
I have seen your spirit when you create.
I have witnessed Life underneath a magnifying glass.
And I have felt Life's spark in those billowing hourglass sands.

So you say you do not believe in God.
And I fully respect and accept that.
But can you believe in this:
-----Inhale--------Exhale-----

Can you believe in *This*?   —*Summer 2012*

If you enjoyed this book of poetry,
check out Karen Neverland's philosophy book:

As Within, So Without:
Love Yourself, Love the World

Our external world is a reflection of our internal world. We interpret
and project a world on the outside that we believe on the inside. For
many of us, this means a world of suffering and hardship.

As Within, So Without: Love Yourself, Love the World is a philosophy that
explains how loving ourselves transforms the world. This book draws
from spirituality, science, religion, and psychology to form a simple
theory on how we can delve in and heal ourselves. When we
experience Unconditional Love within, we experience it without.
When we truly love ourselves, we truly love the world.

Visit her online at www.karenneverland.com.

www.ingramcontent.com/pod-product-compliance
Lightning Source LLC
Chambersburg PA
CBHW071945100426
42736CB00042B/2140